THE CASTES CUSTOMS, MANNERS AND LITERATURE OF THE TAMILS

SIMON CASIE CHITTY

GYAN

Published by

Gyan Publishing House
5, Ansari Road
Daryaganj, New Delhi-110002
Phone: 011-47034999, 9811692060
E-mail: books@gyanbooks.com

Distribution Network
gyanbooks.com
India, USA, Canada, UK, Australia, France

ISBN : 978-81-212-4505-0 (HB)
First Published, 1934

2nd Impression 2020

Printed at: Gyan Press, Delhi.

FOREWORD

By

Dr. S. C. Paul

M.R.C.S. (Eng.), M.D., C.M. (Madras), F.R.C.S. (Eng.), L.R.C.P. (Lond.), M.C.B.R.A.S.

It is very gratifying to see that a grand-daughter of Simon Casie Chitty has come forward to rescue from oblivion the works of such a talented and learned author. Perhaps very few of the present generation are aware of the numerous writings of Simon Casie Chitty, who even in his day was considered a man of versatile genius. His activities extended over a wide field displaying a keen insight and study of Oriental languages and Historical researches. He was an ardent antiquarian and was well versed in the flora and fauna of the Island.

Born on the 27th of March 1807, almost at the beginning of British Rule in this island, his life appears one of intense literary and intellectual activity, while he continued to perform his public duties as a Government Servant so efficiently that he secured rapid promotions in the Service. While holding the appointment of Mudaliyar of Calpentyn he conceived the idea of compiling the first gazetteer on Ceylon. He communicated his intention to Sir Robert Wilmot Horton who was then Governor of Ceylon and received from him a most encouraging letter assuring him of every encouragement and assistance in the project which might be in his power to afford. This work was published in 1834, exactly a hundred years ago today, and served as a model to many later publications. His work in this direction was so much appreciated that His Excellency the Governor nominated him to a seat in the Legislative Council as at that time no educated Ceylonese could be found outside the Government Service for nomination to the unofficial side of the Council. The Secretary of State, however, disapproved the principle involved in these appointments, and Casie Chitty had to revert back to the service. He was then appointed Police Magistrate of Calpentyn and subsequently promoted to the District Judge-ship of Chilaw which post he held till his death at the early age of 54. Within this short period he had published several works covering various departments of literary, historical, antiquarian, religious, philological and scientific researches

FOREWORD (Contd.)

amounting to nearly 50 contributions of great value and learning.

One of the most outstanding works of his is the "Tamil Plutarch" giving the life and writings of all the great authors of Tamil literature beginning with Agastiyar and ending with contemporary writers of his period. Some very original observations were made by him on the writings of the Tamil authors of repute. This is a work which should be preserved for posterity

The present volume entitled "The Castes, Customs, Manners, and Literature of the Tamils" is another one of his distinguished works. Mrs. Gardiner, the granddaughter of the author has rendered a signal service to the Tamils of Ceylon in arranging to publish all the works of her distinguished ancestor.

S. C. PAUL

"Rao Mahal,"
Ward Place,
Colombo.
October, 1934.

CONTENTS

CHAPTER I.

ORIGIN AND COUNTRY OF THE TAMILS

THE Tamils form a considerable portion of Her Britannic Majesty's subjects in the East, and occupy, from their situation, a very important territory in the South of India. Being confounded by the Portuguese with the inhabitants of **Malayalam, Maleiwar,** or **Malabar,** they have in common with them received the appellation of **Malabars**; though the use of it is now gradually wearing away. The Singhalese call them **Demelu,** and in Pali they bear the name of **Damilo.**

Of the epithet **Tamil** it is difficult to trace the Etymology. Mr. Colebrooke, in his Essay on the Sanskrit and Prakrit Languages, *(vide Asiatic Researches, Vol: VII. p. 226)*, observes that "**Tamila, Tamlah** seems to indicate a derivation from **Tamra** or **Tamraparni**, a river of note situated within the limits of **Dravira**;" but this conjecture is, however, founded merely on the analogy the two words exhibit in their sounds. In the Dictionary entitled **Sulamani Nigandu**, the word **Tamil**, besides being a proper appellative, is defined as synonymous with the common nouns ***inimi***, sweetness, and ***neermi***, harmony; both perhaps in reference to the peculiarities of the Tamil language.

From whence the Tamils have derived their origin is a question equally hard to be solved as their name. A supposition has been advanced by the late Professor Rask (*vide Transactions of the Royal Asiatic Society, Vol: III, p. 125*) that they, with the **Telegus**, **Carnalaca** and **Malayalma**, owe their descent to "one great race of men which may be styled **Scythian**", and this it would appear, is countenanced by the tradition that they came from the North, and having supplanted the **Kurumber**, who were the aboriginal tribes established themselves in the Southern parts of India. It should, however, be observed, that the Tamils, like the Egyptians of old, consider themselves the most ancient of mankind, and own no other country as their primitive residence than that which they now inhabit.

The country assigned to the Tamils in the Nigandu is one of the fifty-six **desas** of the Hindu Geographers. Its Sanskrit appellation is **Dravida** or **Dravira**, which the Tamils have changed into **Tiravidam** or **Tiramidum**, conformably to the orthography of their language. The limits of this region, as described by Pavanandi in his Nannool, are marked on the East by the sea, on the West by the Coorg country; on the North by Vengadam or Tripais; and on the South by Cape Comorin, and according to the ancient divisions, it comprehended thirteen **Nadu** or districts, of which one was distinguished by the name of **Shentamil Nadu**, or the district where the polished Tamil was spoken, and the other twelve collectively **Kaduntamil Nadu**, or the district where the vulgar Tamil was spoken.

Mr. Babington, in his preface to the Adventures of Guru Paramartan, pl, speaking of the Tamil language, observes that it is spoken by a population of more than five millions; being current in the Southern portion of the Peninsula of India, throughout the Jaghire, the districts of South Arcot, Salem, Coimbatoor, Combaconum. Taniore, Trichinopoly, Madura,

Dindigul, and Tinnevelly, as well as in many parts of the extensive kingdom of Mysore.

The Tamils are found in Ceylon in the Northern and North-Eastern parts, and their districts extend from the river **Kumukan-ar,** bounding Mahagampattoo, to the Southern limit of Puttalam round by Jaffna Until the change in the division of the Island which were effecte in 1833, the whole of this part of the coast was denominated the Malabar Provinces in contradistinction to the other part which was called The Singhalese Provinces.

The Tamils, as is well known, are not indigenous to Ceylon but emigrated from the opposite coast at different periods; there is however some doubt as to the exact epoch of their first settlement. The great historical work of the Singhalese—The Mahawansa—mentions that **Wijayo** who founded the Singhalese dynasty in Ceylon, B. C. 543, sent for wives both for himself and his seven hundred associates from amongst the Tamils in "**Southern Madhura**" (the kingdom of Pandiya) and they were accompanied by "eighteen officers of state, together with seventy-five menial servants," but it scarcely alludes to any other influx of the Tamils into the Island earlier than the year B. C. 237, when two youths of that nation, named **Seno** and **Guttico**, "powerful in their cavalry and navy" are said to have assumed the government of the country and "righteously reigned for twenty-two years." (*vide Mr. Turnour's Maha Wanso, Vol : 1 p. 51, 127*). In a Tamil poem written by **Kaviraja Varotheiyen**, of which an abridged account is given in the supplement to the **Ceylon Gazette** of November 26, 1831, we find that so far back as the year 512 of the Kali Yug (B. C. 2588) a colony of Tamils was settled on the North-Eastern side of the Island from the Coromandel coast by **Kolakotu Maharaja**, son of **Manunidikanda Chola** king of **Choladesama**, and who built the famous temple in honour of **Koneiswara** at Trincomalie, which was demolished by the Protuguese in 1622. A tradition is also current that about the time the **Kauravas** and **Pandavas** were contesting for the sovereignty of India, and which the learned Orientalist **Wilford** fixes at 1300 years before Christ, the **Tamils** were in possession of the North-West coast of Ceylon, and that their sovereign **Alli Arasani**, likewise called **Sittirankandei** and **Sittiraregei**, who espoused Arjuna, one of the **Pandava** princes, held her court at a place which is at present known by the name of **Koodramalle** and which is supposed to be that named by the Greeks **Hipporus.** Sir Alexander Johnston who visited Koodramalle in 1808 for the purpose of examining "The remains of many very large buildings found there" also mentions in one of his communications to the Royal Asiatic Society *(Vide Transactions, Vol. 1. p. 545)* that he possesses a history of a Queen who reigned over that town and the adjacent country about eighteen hundred or two thousand years ago; but neither in that section of the **Baradam** entitled **Tirthayatrei Padalam,** nor in the **Alliarasane Nataka,** which give some account of the before-mentioned princess, can we find any allusion made to the fact of her having ruled in Ceylon, and we are further infotmed by Mr. Taylor, that her marriage with **Arjuna** is sculptured in full relief on one of the granite pillars which support thc roof of the Choultry built by **Trimala Naickar** at Madura (*vide Oriental Historical Mss. vol. 1. 122*).

It is stated, that when Wijayo landed in Ceylon, he found it inhabited by the **Yakkhos** or **Yakkhinis** who were not however demons as their name implies, but merely worshippers of demons like the "savages, who are scattered amongst the forests of Malabar, and in the woods and mountains of the Carnatic" (*vide Maha Wanso, vol. 1. Index and Glossary, p. 30; Abbe Duboi's Description of India, p. 452*) and if a conjecture may be hazarded, I should be inclined to suspect that they were the remnants of some of the ancient Tamil colonies. The strange story that the **Yakkhini** princess **Kuwene** was born with three breasts, and that one of them disappeared when she married Wijayo seems almost paralleled by that of **Tadatagei-Prattiyar,** the daughter of the king **Malayad-waja Pandiya** who anciently reigned at Madura as recorded in the fourth chapter of the **Tiruvilleiyadel Puranam.**

The Tamil population in the South of India cannot fall much short of eight or nine millions, and in Ceylon it may be estimated at between four and five hundred thousand.

CHAPTER II

DIVISION AND SUB-DIVISIONS OF CASTES

The Tamils are divided into four **Varnas,** or tribes. The first is called **Pirama,** the second **Sattriya,** the third **Vaisiya** and the fourth Sutra; corresponding with the Hindu divisions of Brahmans, Kshatriyas, Vaisiyas, and Sudras.

It did not occur to me, when preparing the former Essay on the classification of the Tamil castes, which was appended to the Ceylon Gazetteer, that there were certain synonymous titles peculiar to each of these tribes. I have since found a list of them, given by Beschi, in his famous Tamil Dictionary entitled **Sadur Agaradi,** and as they indicate the origin, rank and profession of the tribe to which they are appropriated, it may not be amiss to notice them here.

DIVISIONS & SUB-DIVISIONS OF CASTES

The synonyms of the Brahmans are: **Ayenmuhattu Vandore,** those who emanated from the face of Brahma; **Arrutollilaler,** those who have six duties to perform; **Tolukulattore** the worshipping Tribe; **Poosurer,** those who offer **puja** or sacrifice; **Shenti-Valappore,** those who kindle the sacrificial fire; **Vediyer** teachers of the Veda; **Muppuri-noolore,** those who wear the Triple cord; **Irruppirappaler,** the twice born; **Purohiter,** astrologers, **Vedaparagar,** those who bear the vedas; **Parppar** star gazers; **Velviyaler** those who make burnt offerings; **Adivaruner,** those of the first tribe; **Iyer,** teachers, also fathers; **Andaner,** sages; **Uyandore** the exhalted; **Noolor,** framers of the cannons; **Murreiyaver,** lawgivers; and **Marreikodiyore,** those who live under the banner of religion.

Some of the synonyms of the Kshatriyas are: Ayendolvandore, those who emanated from the shoulder of Brahma, **Poopaler,** protectors of the earth, **Kavaler,** the guardians of the people; **Poruner,** warriors; **Kottaver,** the powerful; **Irrai** or **Irreiver,** masters; **Mudelver** or **Taleiver** chiefs, **Narapati,** lords of men; **Poopati,** lords of the earth; **Torapati,** lords of the Chank; **Chakkiri,** lords paramount; and **Mun, Munnar, Munnaver** or **Araser,** kings.

The synonyms of the Vaisiyas are: **Ayenuruvil-Vandore,** those who emanated from the belly of Brahma; **Muttollilore,** those who have three duties to perform; **Ilangkokal,** Juniors of the kings; **Ettyer** or **Ipper,** merchants; **Velalar,** the bountiful; **Karaler,** cultivators; **Munnerpinner,** those who rank below the kings; and **Talalar,** those who possess greatness of mind.

The synonyms of the Sudras are:—**Ayenpadattudittore,** those who emanated from the feet of Brahma; **Munmakkel,** children of the earth; **Ulaver,** ploughmen; **Kalamer,** field labourers; **Vineigner,** manufacturers; **Sadurther,** the fourth; and **Pinnaver,** the last.

The story of the four tribes having derived their origin from the different members of Brahma's body, is wrapt in an allegory, which Abbe Dubois, in his Description of India, Chap. 5 p. 34, endeavours to unravel thus: "The Brahmans, no doubt, being generally engaged in the spiritual concerns of life must have burst from the head of the Creator. Power being the attribute of the Rajas (Kshatriyas) who were ordained to the arduous duties of war; from whence could their origin be derived but from the shoulders and arms of Brahma? The merchants (**Vaisiyas**) solely occupied in providing food, clothing and other necessaries of life, were no less appropriately drawn from the belly of the God; and the plodding Sudras, doomed to the humble drudgery of the field, were shapen out of his feet."

Nothing certain is as yet known respecting the exact period when the classification of the people into castes was effected. It would however appear that the distinction of caste has been in existence in India from long before the commencement of the Christian era; for we find allusions made to it in the **Baradam**, the heroes of which are supposed to have lived 1300 years antecedent to the birth of Christ as we have stated elsewhere.

The following extracts, translated from the 12th Chapter of the **Sulamani Nigandu**, explains the occupations set apart for each Tribe:

" Reading the (Veda) and teaching others to read (them); offering sacrifices and causing them to be offered, giving alms (to the poor) and receiving presents (from the rich) are the six occupations of the Brahmans.

DIVISIONS & SUB-DIVISIONS OF CASTES

"Reading (the Veda) offering sacrifices; giving alms; gathering riches; tending cattle; and tilling the earth are the six occupations of the Vaisiyas.

"Working for the three classes of Vaisiyas in their three occupations, namely, gathering riches, tending cattle and tilling the earth; serving the Brahmans; playing on instruments of music, as drums and pipes; and weaving silk and cotton into cloth, are the six occupations of the Sudras."

It is not to be supposed, that the division among the Tamils ends with the fore mentioned four Tribes only; for each of them is further divided into several **Jatis** or castes, which it will be my business to notice in the four succeeding chapters; though I confess I find it exceedingly difficult to enumerate them with any accuracy, as they vary in the different countries not only in their names and occupations, but also in the order of precedence.

CHAPTER III

DIFFERENT KINDS OF BRAHMANS

The Brahmans are exclusively set apart for the priesthood like the **Levites** among the Hebrews. It is, however, a mistake to suppose that they are required to confine themselves only to the priestly profession ; for the **Vedas** permit them to bear arms, or to carry on merchandize or cultivate the ground, provided they are unable to subsist by their particular duties. "The greater part of the Brahmans in the Lower **Carnatic**," says Buchanan, "follow secular professions. They almost entirely fill the different offices in the collection of revenue, and administration of Justice ; and they are exclusively employed as **Hircaras**, that is guides or messengers, and as the keepers of inns or **choultries**." (*Vide Journey through Mysore, Canara, and Malabar, vol. 1 p. 18.*)

In primitive times there were four **Asramas**, or religious orders, to one of which every Brahman belonged. The first **(Bramachari)** required its members to continue bachelors the whole of their life, and give themselves up wholly to the study of the **Vedas**. The second **(Grahastha)** required its members being in a state of wedlock, to perform the duties towards the Gods and towards the manes as laid down in the **Vedas**, and also to protect the three other orders. The third **(Vanaprastha)** required its members to retire from the world and live in the forests, following the rules of austere devotion assisted by their wives. The fourth **(Sanniyasi)** required its members to forsake mundane affections, and live entirely on alms, and be always engaged in profound meditation. Though these orders have not been formally abrogated in the **Kali** age, yet the two first only are now generally observed but with such modifications, that the title of **Bramachari** is at present given to a young Brahman from the age of seven years, when he assumes the **Poonool**, or triple cord, and enters into his studies, till he is married, which is about the age of sixteen. The **Grahastha** has become an ordinary appellation to every Brahman that is married and has children.

In a marginal note appended by Professor Wilson to his "select specimens of the theatre of the Hindus," vol. II p. 12, thirteen **Gotras**, or families of Brahmans are mentioned, as being enumerated in **Aswalayana Sutra** of the **Rig Veda.** As far as I could ascertain, the Brahmans among the Tamils are divided only into seven **Gotras,** each of which claims its descent from one of the seven **Rishis,** or divine sages, who are **Kasyapa, Atri, Braradwaj, Gautama, Visvamitra, Jamadagni** and **Vashistha** and whom some imagine to have been the seven sons of Japhet! The connection of **Gotra** is entirely in the male line; and a man and woman of the same Gotra never marry together.

The subdivisions of the Brahmans into castes are numerous; and it would be impossible to trace them with any accuracy; differing, as they do, in their names as well as occupations in different parts of the country.

Independently of these distinctions, which are more or less of a civil nature, the Brahmans are divided into three general sects, called the **Smartal,** the **Ayangar** or **Vaishnaval,** and the **Madual.**

The Smartal sect forms about one half of the Brahmans. Its members worship **Siva**; but they consider **Brahma, Vishnu,** and **Siva** to be the same God, assuming different persons as the creator, preserver and destroyer of the universe.

They rub the asnes of cow-dung every morning on the crown of the head, forehead, neck, breast, arms, back, and knees.

The **Vaishnaval** sect forms about three tenths of the Brahmans. Its members abhor Siva, calling him the chief of the **Rakshasas**, or demons, and worship only **Vishnu.** They wear vertical marks on the forehead, made with white, yellow, or red clay.

The **Madual** sect forms the remaining two tenths of the Brahmans. Its members wear the same vertical marks on the forehead as those of the Vaishnaval; but they worship both Vishnu and Siva.

"A difference of sect does not properly constitute a difference of caste, as the son of a Smartal may become a worshipper of **Vishnu,** and the contrary; such changes are not common. The **Smartal** and **Madual** eat together, and intermarry, although the one worship Siva and the other **Vishnu**; the **Sri Vaishnavam** or **Ayangar** will not marry, nor eat with a Madual although they both worship **Vishnu**; and still less will they have any communication with a **Smartal** which arises, however, not from any difference in caste, but from a hatred of the doctrines entertained by these sects," (*Brahman's Journey through Mysore, Canara, and Malabar, vol 1. p. 309)*.

The Brahmans are found almost in every town in the South of India and in the year 1836, their number in the collectorate of Madura alone was estimated at 39,201. In Ceylon, however, they are confined only to Jaffna, and their total scarcely exceeds a few thousands.

The Brahmans in general bear a very striking affinity to the ancient Egyptians both in their religious and civil institutions, and I think it may not be out of place here to add an extract from my observations on the subject, which appeared in the **Colombo Friend** No. 5 of 1838.

" The Egyptian Triad, or Osiris, Horus and Typhon were brought forth by the same parent, though Horus is believed to have sprung from the mysterious embraces of **Osiris** and **Isis** before their birth. The Brahmans believe that **Brahma, Vishnu** and **Siva**, who form their triad, were the three sons of **Adi Sakti**, or the first power. In the Bhagavata it is however mentioned that **Brahma** arose from the lotus which sprang from the navel of **Vishnu**.

The colour of Osiris was black, Horus white, and Typhon red. Brahma is represented of a red, Vishnu of a black and Siva of a white complexion.

The Egyptians considered Osiris and his consort Isis as their supreme deities. In the mythology of the Brahmans, Siva and Parvati occupy the first rank, under the titles of Ishwara and Iishina.

As Osiris was also considered the sun, so is Ishawara ; hence his titles of **Andakaribu** or "the enemy of darkness," and **Viyomakesa** or " the lord of the firmanent." It deserves notice, that as Osiris signifies "many eyed," so **Sahasraksha** an epithet applied to **Indra**, the regent of the firmament, who in some respects coalesces in character with him, implies " a thousand eyed."

The Egyptians symbolized **Osiris** under the type of a bull. The Brahmans, though they do not do so with their **Ishwara** yet represent him as riding on a bull.

The Egyptians worshipped **Anubis** in the form of a dog ; he was, according to the sacred fables the son of **Osiris**, but illegitimate. The God **Bahirava**, the son of **Ishwara**, has a dog for his **vahan** or vehicle, hence he is called Gnali-yoorthi, or " The dog rider."

The Egyptians accounted as divinities the **ox Apis**, the dog, the wolf, the crocodile, the ibis, the cat etc., and it was death for any person to kill one of these animals voluntarily. The Brahmans worship the cow, the ox, the bird **Garuda**, the ape Hunuman, and the cobra capella, and the crime of killing any of them is considered the same as that of killing a man. Though the cat is not in the list of their Gods, yet the killing of it is also prohibited as a very heinous sin. **Apis** was also called **Sorapis** or **Serapis.** The Brahmans call the cow of Indra by the name of **Surabbi**; she is said to have been produced by the ocean of milk, when churned by the gods for the amrita or ambrosia.

The Egyptians worshipped the **Phallus**, which was consecrated to **Osiris**. The Brahmans have a similar emblem, called Lingam, worshipped exclusively sacred to Ishwara.

The Egyptians venerated the Nile, and ascribed to its waters a purifying and divine virtue. The Brahmans also venerate the rivers, particularly the Ganges, which effaces sins, how heinous soever, committed by such as bathe in its water.

The Egyptians also revered the lotus, the flower of which was consecrated to Isis and it ornamented the head of Osiris. The Lotus among the Brahmans is sacred to Lakshimi, the consort of Vishnu, and the flower is offered to Brahma.

The Egyptians did not dare to eat leeks, garlic or onions for fear of injuring their gods. The Brahmans also abstain from eating onions.

The Egyptians in a feast of Isis carried her on a chariot with four wheels drawn by her priests. They also carried the image, enclosed in a little shrine made of wood. Both these ways of carrying out their gods in procession are practised by the Brahmans in Jaffna, and on the coast.

The Egyptians held a feast of lights a Sais. On the occasion they hung up by night great number of lamps, filled with oil mixe with salt round every house, the wick swimmin on the surface, and these burned during th whole night. Those who were not present at th solemnity observed the same ceremonies whe ever they happened to be; lamps were lighted that night, not only at Sais, but throughout Egypt *(Herodotus Europe 52)*. The Brahmans also have a similar feast celebrated in the month of **Kartika** (November), when they light up thousands of lamps in their temples and about the streets, and at the doors of their houses. This feast is held in honour of Maha Bali, a giant king who was trodden to death by Vishnu in the disguise of a dwarfish Brahman.

The Egyptians believed in the transmigration of the soul, so do the Brahmans.

The priests of Egypt accounted it unholy to kill any thing which has life, saving what they used in sacrifice *(Herodotus c110 140)* and that it was not till a late period of their history that animal sacrifices were introduced. *(Porphyry, De Abtin Lib: ii et iv)*. The Brahmans respect every thing that has the principle of life, and animal food is totally interdicted among them.

The Egyptians called their high priests "Piromis" (*Herod. Eutupe chap. 163*) which Larcher derives from Brama (Brahma), signifying Brahmans. The Brahmans are called in Tamil "Piramaner" and Brahma "Piramen" for want of the character B in that language.

DIFFERENT KINDS OF BRAHMANS

The Egyptian priests had the exclusive possession of the sacred books, so have the Brahmans with regard to the **Vedas.**

In the classification of castes a striking resemblance is also observable between the Egyptians and the Brahmans. As in Egypt the people were divided into the clergy, the military, the husbandmen, and the artificers, so we have in India the Brahmans, the Kshatriyas, the Vaisiyas and the Sudras."

To return from this digression, the Brahmans are divided into seven **gotras** or families, each claiming for its founder one of the seven Rishis or sages of antiquity, who were **Kasyapa, Atri, Baradwaja, Gautama, Visevamitra, Jamadagni** and **Vashistha,** and whom some imagine to have been the seven sons of Japhat!

The Rev. Philippus De Melho, whose merits as a Tamil scholar are too well known to require any comment here, in his "Table of castes" written in Dutch in the year 1786, has noticed however only the three following divisions among the Brahmans, perhaps from an idea that all the rest are merged in them :—

DIFFERENT KINDS OF BRAHMANS

1. The race of **Agni**, or the worshippers of fire.
2. The race of **Kasyapa**, or the worshippers of Siva.
3. The race of **Baradwaja**, or the worshippers of Vishnu.

Besides these septenary and triple divisions, the Brahmans are split into several others, of which however no accurate list could be procured. There are some classes mentioned in the **Jati Nool** as comprised under the general denomination of Brahmans; but they appear to have originated from the unhallowed unions of the Brahmans with other tribes in remote times.

Independently of these classifications, there is another distinction of the Brahmans, namely, **Vaishnavas** and **Saivas**; the former, as followers of Vishnu, draw three perpendicular lines in the middle of their forehead with red ochre, and the latter as followers of **Siva**, rub their forehead, neck, breast, arms, etc., with the ashes of cow dung.

With few exceptions, the Brahmans are found almost in every town in the South of India and in 1836 their number in the collectorate of

Madura alone was estimated at 39,201. In Ceylon however they are confined only to Jaffna, and their total scarcely exceeds a few thousands. They are all **Saivas** ; but in consequence of their ancestors having been converted to the Christian faith, their brethren on the continent consider them as a deteriorated race.

CHAPTER IV

DIFFERENT KINDS OF KSHATRIYAS

The Kshatriyas, as we have already observed, constitute the tribe of warriors, and were at one time the exclusive possessors of regal authority. It is the general opinion, that none of this Tribe exists in the present age, the whole having been exterminated by **Parasu Rama,** the sixth **avatar** or incarnation of Vishnu ; but there are several families still in the South of India, who claim filiation with them.

Before we proceed to notice the different classes of Kshatriyas, it may not be improper here to insert the following particulars concerning the appendages of royalty, **etor,** as enumerated in the 12th chapter of the **Sulamani Nigandu,** and in the **Sadur Agaradi.**

The six endowments **(Arasarangam)** of a king, viz :

DIFFERENT KINDS OF KSHATRIYAS

1. **Mantri**, (wise) ministers.
2. **Nadu**, (a strong) population.
3. **Aran**, fortifications
4. **Porul**, (a good) revenue
5. **Paddei**, (a powerful) army
6. **Natpoo**, friends and alliances.

The three properties (Gunam) of kings: viz:

1. **Toonqamei**, decision
2. **Kalvi**, learning
3. **Tunivoo**, prowess

The four virtues which add splendour (Oli) to a king, viz:

1. **Kodei**, liberality
2. **Talsiyali**, benignity
3. **Shenkole**, justice.
4. **Kudiyombel**, care of his subjects

The ten things (Tsangam) appertaining to a king in right of his office, and on which his prosperity rests, viz:

1. **Malei**, Mountains
2. **Aar**, Rivers

3. **Nadu,** Country
4. **Oor,** Cities
5. **Mâlei,** Garlands
6. **Pari,** Horses
7. **Kari,** Elephants
8. **Murasu,** Drums
9. **Kodi,** Flags
10. **Shenkole,** Sceptre

The four acts, in which the power **(Vallamei)** of a king consists, viz:

1. **Eyattal,** the act of making acquisitions
2. **Eet'tai,** the act of collecting his revenues
3. **Kattal,** the act of securing them
4. **Vahuttal,** the act of distributing them

The twenty-one distinguishing marks (Sinnam) of a king, viz:

1. **Mudi,** crown
2. **Kudei,** umbrella
3. **Kaveri,** whisk made of Tibet cow's ta
4. **Toti,** hook with which elephants ar goaded

5. **Murasu**, drum
6. **Chakra**, a sort of discus
7. **Yanei**, elephant
8. **Kodi**, flag
9. **Mathil**, fort
10. **Toranam**, triumphal arches
11. **Neer kudam**, water-pot
12. **Malei**, garlands
13. **Chank**, voluta graves
14. **Kaddel**, sea
15. **Makara**, alligator
16. **Amei**, tortoise
17. **Eneikkaiyel**, two corps
18. **Singam**, lion
19. **Deepam**, torches
20. **Idapam**, bull
21. **Aasanam**, throne

The five different descriptions of attendants (**kulu**) on kings, viz :

1. **Mantri**, ministers
2. **Purohiter**, priests
3. **Senapathi**, generals
4. **Toother**, envoys
5. **Saraner**, spies

DIFFERENT KINDS OF KSHATRIYAS

The eight different assistants **(Tuneiver)** of kings, viz:

1. **Mantri,** Ministers
2. **Karmadikarer,** courtiers
3. **Suttam,** kinsfolks
4. **Kadei-kappaler,** door-keepers
5. **Nagara makkel,** citizens of the capital
6. **Padei taaver,** commanders of the army
7. **Irnle maraver,** cavaliers
8. **Yanei veerer,** warriors mounted on elephants

The five confidential servants **(Uruthichchuttam)** of a king viz:

1. **Natpaer,** companions
2. **Andanaer,** Brahmans
3. **Madeitoliler,** cooks
4. **Maruttuvakaleigner,** physicians
5. **Nimitigappulaver,** bards, also foretellers of future events.

According to the traditions of the Tamils, and from what appears in the few fragments of their early history which have been preserved in the several **puranical** legends, there were formerly three different **dynasties of Tamil kings** in the South of India, named **Sera, Chola** and **Pandiya,** and they continued to reign separately, and at the same time, over three distinct kingdoms, from so far back as 1500 years before the birth of Christ, until they were overthrown by the Telugu sovereigns of **Vijayanagara,** in the period between A. D. 1490 and 1515. The kingdom governed by the Seras was called Seramandalam ; that by the Cholas was called Cholamandalam ; and that by the Pandiyas was called the Pandimandalam, and their boundaries are explained in their stanzas, ascribed to the celebrated Poetess **Auveiyar,** of which the following is a translation.

"On the North is the holy place **Palani,** on the East is **Chongodu ;** on the West **Kolikoodie** (Calicut); and on the South is the margin of the sea, in all eighty **kadams** (equal to 800 miles); these are called the boundaries of the Sera kingdom."

"On the East is the sea; on the South is the river **Vellar** which overflows its banks; on the West is **Kottie karei ;** and on the North is the river **Pennei** of the **Yenad** country, in all twenty four **kadams** (equal to 240 E. miles); these are called the boundaries of the **Chola** kingdom."

DIFFERENT KINDS OF KSHATRIYAS

" South of the river **Vellar**, north of **Kanni** (cape Comorin), East of **Peruveli**, and West of the wave abounding sea, in all sixty four kadams (equal to 640 E. Miles), these are called the boundaries of the Pandiya kingdom."

It would appear that these kingdoms, as well as their sovereigns, were known to the Greeks and Romans; for Sera is mentioned by their writers, under the names of **Cupporbottes**, **Celabothrus** or **Cerebothom**; **Chola** or **Cholamandalam**, under the names of **Sorae** or **Sormandulam** and **Pandimandalam** or **Madura**, under the names of **Pandionis Mediterranae** and **Modusa regia Pandionis Modura**; and we are also informed, that when the Greeks were driven entirely from India, **Pandian** sent an embassy to Augustus Cæsar at Rome to propose entering into an alliance with him, (*vide Bartolomeo's Voyage to the East Indies p. 57, 305. Robertson's Disquisition concerning Ancient India, Sec. 11, p. 73. Vincent Periplus of the Erythrean sea, vol. II. p. 401, 408 etc.*)

It is necessary to notice here, that what I asserted in a former essay concerning the Tamil origin of the founder of the Singhalese dynasty is an error, into which I was led by the followin account given by Mr. Melho in his Table of Tamil castes. **Wijayo** it appears, derived his descent from a royal family that had anciently reigned over some part of the Northern circars; but his queen, however, was a Tamil princess, the daughter of one of the Kings of the **Pandiy** dynasty, to whom Wijayo paid an annual tribute of chanks and pearls, in value two lacks. **(Mahawanso chap. vii).**

It is, perhaps, not unknown, that there are at present in the Southern Carnatic, several chieftains called **Polugars** who until very lately exercised a sort of regal authority over their respective polloms or clans; but it should here be remarked, that none of them belonged to the Kshatriya tribe, though they sometimes pretend to trace their pedigree to the ancient kings. The polygarships appear to be of a modern date, being created under the Government of the Naiks of Madura, to aid them in repelling the attacks of the Mohamedans.

The kings who ruled in Jaffna, were descended from the **Chola** race, but by a Brahman mother, and hence they took upon them the ambiguous title of **Ariya vamisem** to signify both sides of their parentage; for the word **Ariyen** is a synonym for a priest as well as for the Cholas. These kings were very powerful and had at one time extended their conquests over the whole of the North-west coast of Ceylon, and thrown up fortifications at Colombo, Negombo and Chilaw. It is stated in the **Kailasa Malei,** that their dynasty was founded in the year 101 B. C. and it lasted as late as 1591 A. D. when the Portuguese made themselves masters or Jaffna.

There is a very extraordinary race of people in Jaffna, who claim their descent from the offspring of the before mentioned kings by the ladies of their harems, as we have stated in the former essay. They are called **Maddapallis** of which the etymology is much disputed. The Velales, with whom they have a constant jarring about precedence, derive it from the word **Maddapalli** or kitchen, where they say it was the duty of the mothers of the Maddapalli to attend, but the **Maddapallis** on the other hand assert it to have emanated from **Maddappam,** a term applied in the **Nigandu** to a village that has the presidency over five hundred smaller ones, their ancestors having been the chieftains of such villages in ancient times. There are two distinctions of **Maddapallis,** namely, **Maddapallis** and **Kumara Maddapallis,** and if I am rightly informed, they are only to be found in Jaffna.

CHAPTER V

THE DIFFERENT KINDS OF VAISIYAS

The Vaisiyas compose the nobility of the country, though they have now in some degree lost most of the rights and privileges which they formerly enjoyed.

There are three principal divisions of Vaisiyas, which are named and arranged, in the **Sadur Agaradi**, as follows :—

1. Tana Vaisiyas or merchants.
2. Poo Vaisiyas or husbandmen.
3. Ko Vaisiyas or herdsmen.

The Tana Vaisiyas, excepting such as now fill offices under the Government, are wholly employed in carrying on mercantile affairs; and in their opinion a good merchant should possess the following eight qualities viz :—

DIFFERENT KINDS OF VAISIYAS

1. To know proper prices
2. To collect goods
3. To divide his profits fairly
4. To pursue his speculations, though not always attended with success
5. To inform himself, with a view to trade, of the customs of different countries, the disposition of the people, and the seasons favourable to his schemes
6. To keep secret the real state of his concerns
7. To go quickly with his trade, waiting with patience for suitable success
8. To close his business every day before sunset, and retire to his house in proper time.

(Vide Kottler's Tamil Dictionary)

The Tana Vaisiyas are sometimes called **Vanigar** and **Vaniber.** In ancient times, they had also the exclusive right to use the title of Chetty as an honorary affix to the name, but it is now, however, extended to almost every person who trades, including the members of certain tribes of weavers, oil makers and fishmongers, as will be shown in a future chapter.

DIFFERENT KINDS OF VAISIYAS

It should be observed here, that the author of the **Maha Wanso** mentions the Tana Vaisiyas under the name of Setthi and we are informed by him, that "the illustrious **Thero** Mahindo," who introduced the Buddhist religion into Ceylon, as born of a female of their tribe. (*Vide Mr. Turnour's Maha Wanso. p. 76*). In the **Tiruvileyadel Puranam**, two different apparitions of Siva, in the form of **Chetty**, are related to have taken place at Madura during the reigns of the Pandiya kings.

The names of the sub-divisions of the Tana Vaisiyas are in order as follows :—

1. Kuveripoompattarattu Chetties
2. Elelie Chetties
3. Ilyattukudi Chetties
4. Cholapurattu Chetties
5. Puliyenkudi Chetties
6. Poovallukudi Chetties
7. Tiruvappoor Chetties
8. Karuppoor Chetties
9. Sittakkattu Chetties
10. Kaverei Chetties
11. Valayel Chetties
12. Manjappattu Chetties

DIFFERENT KINDS OF VAISIYAS

The Poo Vaisiyas are commonly known and distinguished by the appellation of **Velaler**, from the **Velamei**, or cultivation, in which they are occupied; and the late Mr. Ellis, in his learned commentary on the **Cural**, alluding to them observes—" The Tamil nation may be considered as chiefly agricultural, originally, perhaps, wholly, so far, though various manufactures existed in the provinces to which the dominion of the ancient Tamil princes extended, the several castes by which these were conducted were, by the ancient institutions of the country, in absolute subjection to their cultivating tribes; the Caniyatchicarer, or Lords of the soil, who, however, derived their superiority, not from fictitious incidents, but from the rights of the plough. Intercourse with foreign nations, the extension of commerce, and other circumstances have in later times, materially altered the manners of the older times and infringed the privileges of the landed proprietors, but they have not been able to prevent a lively tradition of them remaining, and this has given origin to the dissertations between the factions denominated **Valang caiyar** and **Idung caiyar**, or, as commonly though improperly called, **the right and left hand castes**; the former including the whole of the agricultural tribes, who endeavour, under a different order of things, to maintain their ancient pre-eminence; the latter, including chiefly the trading and manufacturing tribes, who endeavour, and in modern days greatly with success, to evade it."

The names of the sub-divisions of the **Poo Vaisiyas** are in order as follows :—

1 Karkatta Velaler
2 Tuluwa Velaler
3 Choliya Velaler
4 Kondeikatti Velaler
5 Korukkie Velaler
6 Sembenattie Velaler
7 Kudikal Velaler
8 Aaranattu Velaler
9 Arumpukatti Velaler

The Ko Vaisiyas have several titles peculiar to them such as, Kopuler or cow-keepers; Amuther or milkmen; Toruver or herdsmen, and Kanaver or foresters; but their common designation, however, is Ideiyer or posters, and that in consequence of their inhabiting woody situations **(mullei-nilam)**, they are also sometimes called **Mullei-nilamakkel** or men of the woody land.

The names of the sub-divisions ot Ko Vaisiyas are in order as follows :—

1 Malei Ideiyer
2 Valei Ideiyer
3 Katkat Ideiyer
4 Anjali Ideiyer
5 Namakara Ideiyer
6 Sivishar Ideiyer

CHAPTER VI

OF THE DIFFERENT KINDS OF SUDRAS

The Sudras, who are the last of the four grand divisions, constitute by far the bulk of the Tamil nation, and are divided into several castes, all distinct and not allowed to intermarry with each other.

Though the Sudras are, according to their original institution, bound to work for the three different descriptions of Vaisiyas, yet the whole of their tribe is not considered as being wholly so; for it would appear that out of the many sub-divisions which it comprehends, only eighteen have been selected and appointed exclusively for this purpose, under the appellation of **Kudimakkel** or servants of the public.

The following list contains the names of the castes forming the community of Kudimakkel :—

DIFFERENT KINDS OF SUDRAS

1 Navider, barbers

2 Oacher, heralds who announce marriages and deaths

3 Koller, blacksmiths

4 Tattar, goldsmiths,

5 Kannar, brasiers,

6 Tatcher, Carpenters.

7 Kal Tatcher, stone cutters

These five last castes of artificers pretend to have Viswakarma for their founder, and are collectively called Kammaler. There is a very interesting tradition that anciently they all lived closely united together in a fort built of load-stone at **Mantai** (*Mantote near Manar*), and accumulated immense treasure by their respective trades; but having given offence to certain kings by their contemptuous behaviour, their fort was burnt down to the ground through the instrumentality of the courtezans of a temple, and themselves almost extirpated. (*Vide Journal of the Asiatic Society of Bengal, Vol. vii, p. 411, and also the Tamil poem entitled* **Kalingattu parani.**)

8 Valaiyar, game keepers

9 Panar, tailors

10 Ennei Vaniyar, oil makers
11 Elei „ fruit sellers
12 Pai „ shop keepers
13 Kavelpalli, watchmen
14 Poomalaikarer, flower sellers
15 Vettiyar, who burn the dead
16 Kusaver, potters
17 Veerakudiyar, who blow chanks
18 Vannar, washermen

This list, though framed according to a tanza in the 12th chapter of the Nigandu differs onsiderably from the one given by Ramaswamy Naidu, in his remarks on the Revenue system of Fort St. George (*Vide Jl. R. A. S. vol. 1. p. 298*), not only in the names and occupations of the **Kudimakkel**, but also in their relative rank, and it is, perhaps, proper here to insert an extract from it for comparison.

"1 A Karnam who keeps all accounts belonging to the village

2 A Kavel or Kavelgarer whose duty it is to watch the boundaries of the village, crops stacks, maps and other property of the inhabitants in the village.

3 A Karuman or blacksmith

DIFFERENT KINDS OF SUDRAS

4 A Tatchen or carpenter

5 A Tattan or Goldsmith

6 A Cannan or Brass-smith

7 A Kal tatchen or stone cutter

8 A Kushavan or pot-maker

9 A Navidan or Barber

10 A Vannan or Washerman

11 A Paniseiven or Virakudian, literally a workman who attends on the Head Cultivator of the village and announces all marriages and deaths to the community

12 A Valluven, or tailor, sews the clothes of the cultivators and prays at festivals and at the time of measuring the crops

13 A Vaniyan or Oilman

14 A Parvaniyan or Chetty who keeps a shop in the village

15 A Yelavaniyan or Gardener

16 A Valayan, Fisherman or boatman whose business is to open and shut the sluices of the tanks and is employed at the ferry in cases where the village happens to be situated on the banks of a river. He also fishes in the tanks etc. and sells the fish in the village.

17 A Vochan whose office is to perform puja in the pagoda of the village deity and to

carry a firepot on his head when any dispute happens.

18 Toty, Kurumbokutti or Vettiyan who is Parian by caste who is employed in measuring all the heaps of grains and carrying letters and money in his first capacity; in the second he waters the fields and in the third buries the dead."

Ramaswamy Naidu ascribes the selection and appointment of the Kudimakkal to the Chola prince Adanda Chakkaravarti who colonised the country called Tondamandalam and hence it is I suppose that the law by which their rights and privileges are regulated, has obtained the name of Tondamandalavarisei or the rules of Tondamandalam.

The other subdivisions of the Sudras are too numerous to be enumerated with any accuracy and there are always disputes in adjusting their order of precedence. The following list however has been drawn up from a careful comparison of the different native catalogues of castes in existence and also from the information furnished by several respectable individuals.

DIFFERENT KINDS OF SUDRAS

1 Agambadiyar
2 Maravar
3 Kallar
4 Nattambadi
5 Vallambar, the same as Malayeembar
6 Palli
7 Tottiyar

These seven castes of cultivators are to be chiefly met within the Carnatic where they form several Palliams or clans headed by certain chieftains styled Polygars similar to the title Zemindars in the Nothern Circars.

8. Komattys, Dealers in gold and pearls
9 Paravar (Parawas)
10 Pattanavar
11 Padeikarer
12 Karreiyar
13 Palli Ville
14 Sembadavar
15 Timilar
16 Mukuwar (Mukuwas)
17 Kadeiyar
18 Paramber

These ten last castes are fishermen and boatmen and assume the title of **Kuru Kulam** or the race of Kuru the Genius who presides over the planet Jupiter. In the Nigandu they are collectively called Neithanilamakkal from their living on the sea shore.

19 Salupper, wooden drapers ?

20 Tather, who exhibit comedies, farces and puppet shows

21 Veder, huntsmen or hunters

22 Mutchiyer, painters

23 Seder
24 Kaikkoler
25 Saliyer
26 Sinoyer
} Different sorts of weavers.

The dancing girls attached to the temples in the South of India mostly belong to the Kaikkolar caste and are either devoted to this state which is by no means considered ignominious by their parents or the descendants of those who have been so devoted. Their male offspring are instructed in the use of the cymbal and tabor, the clarion trumpet and various loud sounding instruments, and are the musicians of the temples. **Ellis.**

DIFFERENT KINDS OF SUDRAS

27 Uppalavar, salt makers

28 Otter, the same as upparaver, pond diggers

29 Tanakkarar, Elephant keepers

30 Kuraver, like the gypsies in Europe these people " wander up and down under pretence of telling fortunes, coming diseases etc., abuse the people, trick them out of their money and steal all they can come at." Some however occasionally employ themselves in transporting salt from the sea coast to the interior on the backs of asses; others manufacture wicker baskets and bamboo mats.

31 Jruler, Woodmen

32 Kurumber, probably the descendants of the aboriginal inhabitants of the peninsula of India; they keep sheep and weave a sort of coarse blankets from their wool.

33 Kowiyar, formerly they were slaves to the Velaler in Jaffna and used to work for them in their fields but latterly they have become emancipated

34 Siviyar, palanquin bearers

35 Shanar } Toddy drawers
36 Nalavar }

DIFFERENT KINDS OF SUDRAS

37 Valluver, Soothsayers—also priests of the Parriar tribe

38 Kotiyer, Weavers of the lower order

39 Chakkilyer, Cobblers

40 Parier, Tom tom beaters

41 Paller, Ploughmen of the lower order

The following is an enumeration of the different distinctions or **branch castes** of the beforementioned castes.

No. 5 of the 1st Division **Kannar—**

There are two distinctions viz :

1 Kottukannar who work the metal beating it out with a hammer

2 Vappu Kannar, who melt and cast the metal in a mould

No. 18 of do – **Vannar**

There are four distinctions viz :—

1 **Velvannar**, who wash for the high castes

2 Neela Vannar who dye blue cloths

3 Saya Vannar who dye red cloths

4 Podara Vannar who wash for the low castes

This last is also called Turumba Vannar.

No. 5 of the second Division—Tottiyar

There are nine divisions viz :—

DIFFERENT KINDS OF SUDRAS

1 Sellavar
2 Tokilavar
3 Kottavar
4 Peruvar
5 Maikavar
6 Tiyuvar
7 Kiddeivar
8 Ottiyavar
9 Paddi-var

The Tottiyar worship a particular Goddess called Chakka Devi. They serve as soldiers when required and at other times cultivate lands or stroll about the country telling fortunes and playing on a sort of plate.

No. 9 of Do—**Parawas**

There are 13 distinctions viz :—

1 Headmen
2 Dealers in cloth
3 Divers for pearls
4 Sailors
5 Divers for chanks
6 Divers for coral
7 Packers of cloth for carriage
8 Catchers of Tortoises

9 Catchers of sharks and other fish
10 Catchers of porpoises
11 Palanquin bearers
12 Messengers
13 Catchers of crabs

The Parawas without a single exception are Christians of the Church of Rome to which they were converted by the celebrated missionary Francis Xavier and his colleagues. All of them have, in compliment to the Portuguese by whom they were freed from the oppressive yoke of the Muhamedans adopted their surnames, and in order to distinguish themselves from the other tribes shave their heads quite close and wear large mustachios.

Their chief styled Jadi-Taleiven resides at Tutocoryn and under the Dutch Government he enjoyed many important privileges and immunities besides the title of Prince of the seven Harems.

For a minute account of this interesting race see my "Remarks on the origin and history of the Parawas" published in the JL. of A. S. No. vii.

DIFFERENT KINDS OF SUDRAS

No. 16 of Do—**Mukuwas**

There are seven distinctions viz :—

1 Pichanda Vageiyar
2 Nallanda „
3 Pala Vageiyar
4 Koita Vageiyar
5 Kalanga „
6 Mudivilungu Pandiyataver
7 Vilungonna Vageiyar

It should be observed that these distinctions are confined only to the Mukuwas in Ceylon who disdain the idea of being classed with the piscatory tribes in consequence of the kings of Kandy, by whom they were employed to catch elephants, having conferred on them the privileges of the higher orders and selected from among them twelve members for the courts of Justice at Puttalam.

No. 17 of Do—**Kadaiyar**

There are two distinctions viz :—

The first fish and in Ceylon dig for chaya roots.

The second prepare Chunam by burning sea shells.

DIFFERENT KINDS OF SUDRAS

No. 35 of Do—**Shanar**

There are Eight distinctions viz :—

1 Velan Shanar or husbandmen

2 Kaitpoora „ or dealers in small wares

3 Kalla „ or potters

4 Eaku (ee?) „ or bullock drivers

5 Tennamatta „ or toddy drawers from cocoanut trees

6 Panaimatta „ or toddy drawers from palmyra trees

7 Pallavaraya „ or palankeen bearers

8 Eeluva „ or distillers of spirits

There are some other castes mentioned in the Nigandu namely Marutwar or medical practitioners ; **Tunner** or skin dressers ; **Ulleiyar** or who find out lucky positions for wells, Yalpanar or minstrels ; **Aripper** or those who sift the dust of the goldsmith ; Urcikarar or scabbard makers, Soover or butchers ; Nataker or dancers ; Kuyilawer or Kuyilwanar or who play on stringed instruments ; Paunuwer or horsekeepers and Kalayar or rope dancers ; but whether or not they are still existing as distinct tribes in any part of the Tamil country I have not been able to ascertain.

CHAPTER VII.

OF THE MIXTURE OF CASTES

It is generally acknowledged that originally the Sudras had not so many subordinate castes among them as they have at present and that the greater part of those which we have enumerated in the previous chapter spring from the inter marriages of the established tribes before there were any barriers to such promiscuous intercourse. These mixed races were at first regarded as the scum of the society and placed beyond its pale under the general appellation of **Sankara Jati**; but in course of time the sovereigns of the country formed them into as many different castes of mechanics and tradesmen as were requisite for the service of the Public and incorporated them with the Sudras. Treatises on the genealogy of the mixed castes are very numerous written in the Tamil and Sanskrit languages; among which the one under the title of Jatebeda Nool is considered the best and the following particulars have been chiefly extracted from it.

There are four sets of mixed castes namely :—

1 Anulomer or those whose fathers were of a high caste and their mothers of a low one.

2 Prithilomer or those whose fathers were of low caste and their mothers of a high one.

3 Andaralar or those whose fathers were Anulomer and their mothers Prithilomer.

4 Viratthsiyar (?) or those whose fathers were Prithilomer and their mothers Anulomer.

The first set comprises the following castes viz :—

1 Maruthevar
2 Kometti
3 Kaikkoler
4 Pai-Vaniyer
5 Elei Vaniyer
6 Oracher
7 Kusaver

The second set comprises the following castes viz :—

1 Seder
2 Saliyer
3 Seniyer
4 Ennai-Vaniyer

5 Yalpaner
6 Mutchiyer
7 Kavelpalle
8 Vedar
9 Karraiyar
10 Valeiyer
11 Navider
12 Tather (?)
13 Kalayer
14 Ureikarer
15 Shanar
16 Vannar
17 Parriar

The third and fourth sets comprise the following castes viz :—

1 Kollar
2 Tattar
3 Kannar
4 Tatcher
5 Kal-tatcher
6 Poomalei karar
7 Parawas
8 Pattanaver
9 Palliville

10 Kadeiyer
11 Iruler
12 Chakkiliyer
13 Vettiyar

It should be mentioned here that in some parts of Ceylon it is customary for a person born out of wedlock to be equalized with his father's or mother's caste by performing the ceremony called Pantiyettel. "The individual desiring to be thus equalized must first signify his wishes to the chief and leaders of his caste and upon their assurance that no impediment will be made thereto he raises a Pandal (or booth) in front of his house and decorates it with white cloth. He then personally waits upon every one whom he considers necessary at this feast and invites them severally to his Pandal, where he first undergoes the ceremony of shaving and tying the head cloth, and where a sumptuous entertainment then awaits them, at which he himself presides. In some instances the individual is obliged to pay a sum of money to the temple, and also to make suitable presents to his respective guests; but this is not always the case. When a man has thus been publicly equalized there can be no objection to his associating with any person of his caste.

CHAPTER VIII.

OF THE MARKS OF DISTINCTION AND TITLES

Although the distinction of families by means of coats of arms as observed in Europe is not known to the Tamils, yet certain castes among them have each a distinguishing banner or **Virrudu-Kodi** with the device of some animal or other object painted on it; and this they carry in their bridal processions. They have also each a garland or malei wreathed with a particular description of flowers and worn round the head or neck on such occasions.

The following extract from the Nigandu exhibited here in a Tabular form explains the different devices and garlands of flowers appropriated to each caste.

THE MARKS OF DISTINCTION & TITLES

CASTE	DEVICES PAINTED ON THE BANNERS	FLOWERS USED FOR THE GARLANDS
Brahmans	A Swami	Nymphaea nelumbo
Sera Kings	A Bow	Borassus flabelliformis
Chola Kings	A Tiger	Bauhima Tomentosa
Pandiya Kings	A Fish	Melia azadirachta
Tana Vaisiyers	A Lion	Cumimum Cyminum
Poo ,,	A Plough	Nymphoesa Odorata
Ko ,,	A Kite (?)	Ocymum Savatum
Madapalle	A Bull	Nymphaea Nelumbo
Maravar	A Cudgel	Jasminum grandi florem
Parawas	A Peacock	Nauclea Cadambo
Karreiyar	A Fish	Rhizophora Candel
Pallivilli	A Star	Byonia grandis
Timiler	A Red bul	Michelia champaca
Muckwas	A Swan	Calophyllum inophyllum
Kammalar	A Monkey	——
Navider	A Razor	Corsalpinia pulcherrima
Kaikkoler	A Cummin flower	Nandea Cadamba
Kuraver	A Bow	Nymphaea Nelumbo
Vannar		Phlomis indica
Pariar		Nymphaea Nelumbo

THE MARKS OF DISTINCTION & TITLES

It should be observed that some castes in Ceylon have likewise certain other marks of distinction, which are branded on the hind hips of their cattle in addition to their own initials; these are as under specified.

Tula—A pair of scales, the mark of Tana Vaisiyas

Pasumbei—a figure of six angles, the mark of Poo Vaisiyas

Vilakku—two conical figures placed one upon another, the mark of Ennai Vaisiyer

Savalam—A pike, the mark of Parawas

Makaram—A fish, the mark of Karreiyar

Kuradu—A pair of tongs, the mark of Kammalar

Kodiyung, Kudeiyum—an umbrella surmounted by a flag, the mark of Kadeiyar

Kattirikole—A pair of scissors, the mark of Navider

Kalloo—A quadrangle representing the stone slab on which the washerman beats cloth, the mark of Vannar.

Each caste has a title or Pattoru peculiar to its male members and used as an honorary affix to the names. In the present time however very little attention is paid to the lawful use of these titles, and in Ceylon most of them are applied indiscriminately.

The titles alluded to are as follows and I have placed in juxta position to each the name of the caste to which it belongs.

Brahmans	Iyer
Kshatriyas	Raja
Tana Vaisiyers	Chetty
Poo ,,	Pillai, also Mudali
Ko ,,	Konan
Agambadiyar	Serveikaren
Maravar	Taver
Kallar	Kaudiyen
Naitambadi	Udeiyar
Palli	Padeiyatchi
Tottiyar	Naiken
Kometti	Chetty
Ennei Vaniyar	do
Pai ,,	do
Parawas	Adappen, Adappanar
Pattanavar	Chetty
Sembadavar	Ambalen
Valeiyer	Moopen

THE MARKS OF DISTINCTION & TITLES

Muckwas	Podi
Kaikkolar	Chetty also Mudeli
Seniyer	do
Salupper	do
Navider	Pariary also Pranavopakar
Oacher	Poosari
Siriyar	Pogauden
Shanar	Nadan
Vannar	Ekali
Nalavar	Tannayen
Valluver	Tiru-chamban
Chakkiliyer	Pagadei
Parriar	Sambuven
Paller	Kudukam (or Kudubem ?)

CHAPTER IX.

OF THE PHYSICAL AND MORAL CHARACTERISTICS OF THE TAMILS, THEIR CUSTOMS AND HABITS.

Having enumerated the castes which constitute the Tamil nation I shall now proceed to offer a few remarks on their character, customs and habits.

The Tamils are generally speaking a very active and enterprising race. Though neither so tall nor well made as the Rajput Moguls and Pathans of the north, yet they scarcely yield in point of strength and other physical qualities to the Telugus, Malayalees and Singhalese. Their complexion varies from a dark brown to black, but when not exposed to the heat of the sun, as is the case with the majority of the Brahmans and the women of the superior classes it often approaches to a yellow tint. They have commonly the forehead small, the face thinner, and the hands finer shaped. Their hair and eyes are always black.

The Tamil women are, for the greater part, well looking and often handsome, and Mr. Cordmar (?) speaking of those he met in the country about Trincomalie observes that "their gait is elegant, their countenances are pleasant and comely, exhibiting that species of beauty and placid dignity for which Raphael's paintings are so much celebrated."

There are certain signs which in the opinion of the Tamils as may be gathered from the second chapter of the Nigandu from the verses 108 to 120, characterize a perfect belle and for the sake of the curious I shall here subjoin an explanation of them, translated from a passage in an epic poem describing the person of a Princess. " Her hair was black like the clouds, Voluminous like the moss and glossy like the dark sands of the sea, her forehead and eyebrows were curved like the bow; her eyes were like those of a fawn; her cheeks were smooth like a looking glass; her nose was nicely formed like the Champaka bud: her ear hung loose like a swing; her lips were red like the Tondei fruit; her teeth were bright like pearls; her face was resplendent like the full moon; her voice was sweet as that of a nightingale; her neck was straight like the trunk of an Areka tree, (?) her shoulders were round like the bamboo; her hands were tender like the lotus flower; her fingers were neatly shaped and separated like the fine petals of the Kondal flower; her breasts were conical like the young cocoanut; her belly was flat like the Banian leaf; her waist was slender like that of a lion, her legs were tapering like the probosis of an elephant; her ankles resembled in shape the carp fish; the soles of her feet were soft like the cotton and her gait was graceful as that of a swan."

Respecting the moral character of the Tamils some European writers have given a very unfavourable representation. The reason of this is that the knowledge which the writers in question possessed of the conduct and disposition of the Tamils was extremely limited and I am inclined to believe that they took the vices and defects they observed in the vulgar classes whom they had engaged in their service as butlers, cooks, ayahs or palankeen bearers as the criteria by which to judge of the character of a whole nation. Far be it from me however to assert that the Tamils are exempt from the failings to which human nature is liable in every clime, yet I may confidently aver that there are among them many kind fathers, attentive and tender mothers, obedient and dutiful children, chaste wives, sincere friends, honest traders, industrious husbandmen and faithful servants, and in this assertion it would appear that I am fully supported by the testimony of several other European writers who from the close and familiar intercourse they had with the various classes of the people were perfectly qualified to form a correct estimate of their national character.

I have a great desire to transcribe all the citations I could make on the subject but as I am afraid that it would be trespassing too much on the reader's time I shall content myself with only the few following extracts:-

1. *From Ellis' commentary on the Cural, p. 221.*

" It may with perfect truth be maintained that there is no people more keenly alive to the affections of parent, child and relation, none more ardent in conjugal attachment or more enthusiastic in devotion to the object of their religious veneration than the natives of Southern India. The last fact will perhaps be more readily admitted than the former; but the love of his creatures must, as the predicate of an object in the expression of its identity, be included in the undissembled love of the creator, and he who also feels the latter strongly must therefore be strongly affected towards the former."

2. *From the same p. 672.*

"The women of Southern India are uniformly chaste and temperate by nature. Gentle and timid as they are usually shrinking from observation and exertion, they are nevertheless ardent in their attachments and this disposition directed by education acquires a force which nothing can shake and enables them when actuated by motives of duty or honour to display an energy beyond their sex and a courage which no terrors can daunt. Devoted in body and mind to their domestic and conjugal duties they are affectionate and attentive wives, anxious and tender mothers, and not unfrequently sage and prudent friends."

5. *From Abbe Dubouis's Description of India, p. 195.*

"We ought to add that Hindu women are naturally chaste. In this respect they are undoubtedly of a very different character from what is attributed to them by some authors who have but imperfectly observed their dispositions, and who have no doubt been deceived by the dissoluteness of some females of the nation who connect themselves with Europeans, or of the still greater number who follow the armies. From those particular circumstances, they have ventured to brand them in general with the odious imputation of unchastity. I believe their opinion to be erroneous and I am confident that any person who shall enquire closely and with impartiality into their habitual conduct as I have done will join with me in revering their virtue."

4. *From Hodges' Travels in India, ps. 3 and 4.*

"The natives first seen in India by an European Voyager are Hindoos, the original inhabitants of the Peninsula. In this part of India (Madras) they are delicately framed, their hands in particular are more like those of tender females and do not appear to be what is considered a proper proportion to the rest of the person which is usually above the middle size.

Correspondent to this delicacy of appearance are their manners, mild, tranquil and sedulously attentive; in this last respect they are indeed remarkable, as they never interrupt any person who is speaking but wait patiently till he has concluded; and then answer with the most perfect respect and composure."

5. *From Hoole's Mission to the South of India Part I, p. 61.*

"The Hindus have the character of indolence very freely attributed to them and it may perhaps be merited by many of those who enter the service of Europeans; but the appearance of neatness and comfort about many of the habitations of the merchant, the manufacturer and the farmer, their successful vigilence in observing the seasons for ploughing, sowing etc., the instances of skill and labour observable on every hand in their tanks and conduits for water, and their great personal exertion day and night for the irrigation of their land when the season requires it are sufficient to convince any impartial observer that they deserve the character of an ingenious and industrious people expecially when it is considered that the climate and the circumstances of the country neither require nor generally allow the robust vigour of body possessed by Europeans."

6. *From Colonel Wetli's Military Reminiscences Vol. 1 p. 14.*

"The Tamils of Malabar, a race of Hindoos generally remarkable for mildness of disposition and cleanliness of person are obedient and faithful but not very intelligent or enterprising soldiers."

There is no uniformity with the Tamils in the manner they dispose of their hair. The men for the greater part shave the whole of the hair off leaving only a small tuft (called Kudumi) on the Crown of the head or near the forehead. Mustaches are in fashion but not universally and beards are retained only by the Sanniyasis and Vyragis who have devoted themselves to a life of austerity. The women always wear their hair long which being anointed with cocoanut or gingily oil is either combed and tied up in a knot (called Condei) behind the head or allowed to hang on one side.

Both men and women perforate their ears and this operation is considered indispensable.

Some also make indelible marks of a bluish colour (called Patchei) upon their foreheads and arms and often upon the back of their hands and fingers by puncturing the skin with the point of a needle and then rubbing it over with the juice of the Erytherina Indica or **Dobichos** Tetras-perius. These marks among the heathens represent the weapons and other appendages of their Gods, and among the Christians the subjects of the passion of our Saviour. It is also customary with the women in general to stain their faces and bodies with an infusion of turmeric and to blacken the edges of their eye-lids with a sort of powder resembling the kohkt or kohkl used by the Egyptians for the same purpose (*Vide Lane's Modern Egyptians Vol. 1, p. 41.)*

The national dress of the Tamils is extremely simple, but on the whole graceful and becoming. The dress of the men consists of a cloth (called Somen) of the length of 6 to 12 cubits which being wrapped round the waist one end of it is passed between the legs and fastened behind, while the other end being cast into several folds in front is allowed to hang down as low as the ankles. Over the shoulder another cloth called **Vaity** of the length of four cubits is loosely thrown across and this is often drawn over the head like a hood to keep off the sun when they walk abroad On the head the Brahmans commonly wear a red velvet cap (called Kullah) with flaps that cover the ear, and the rest of the men either put on a turban or tie round the head a square piece of party coloured cloth (called urumal) or a common headkerchief

The dress of the women differs from that of the men in that they wear only a single piece of cloth (called chela) of 18 or 20 cubits in length and often with painted borders. One end of this is folded round the waist two or three times so as to form a sort of tight petticoat falling in front as low as the feet while the other end is tastefully carried over the shoulders so as completely to conceal the body, but leaving the arms bare. The majority of the women in the South of India wear under the chela a bodice (called Ravikkei) either plain or silk embroidered with flowers of gold fitting tight to the shape and long enough to support the breasts; it has short sleeves reaching half way to the elbow.

It has now become the fashion among the Tamil Gentlemen on great occasions to wear over their **Soman** a long robe of muslin (called

Anghi) reaching from their collar bone (where it fits close) to their ankles, and gathered up a little above the waist and bound round the body with a piece of richly embroidered cloth (called Savukkam) folded together several times so as to form a narrow band about the breadth of six or seven inches. On ordinary occasions however they wear instead of this Anghi a short white coat (called Angaraka) which does not descend below the knees and throw over it across the shoulders either a Cashmere shawl or a muslin scarf.

Both these dresses it should be remarked are imitations of the Monguls and Patans. The Tamils however keep up a distinction between themselves and the two former races by fastening their robes to the left side in place of the right.

Among the Parawas and also among the Chetties and Vellalas who follow the Romish creed in Ceylon the habiliment of the men of rank consists of a cloth folded round the waist and a white sleeved waist coat (called Asavi) with gold buttons of a small size in front. Over the Asavi is sometimes worn a jacket (called Maitchattei) differing from a banian only in having very long sleeves tastefully slashed up at the wrists. On the head they have either a turban of a curious shape (Talaichcheelai) or a round cap (called Chantina) made of paste board and lined with velvet.

In Colombo where the manners of the Tamils partake in a greater or less degree of those of Europeans, the national costume among the chetties has undergone considerable modifications. Here the young men instead of the **Soman** wear a pair of loose drawers of striped cotton or silk, tied around the body by a running string and they also sometimes put in under the Angurka which has high collars secured with three gold buttons, a shirt and waist coat. Socks and shoes are also getting in vogue among them and I have reason to think that in the course of some years more they will become almost Anglecised.

The dress of the ladies also assumes a different character from that of those in the South of India and in the Northern part of Ceylon. Their lower attire consists of a piece of cloth of silk (called Camby) which reaches to the feet and the upper one a short shirt (called choli) with buttons at the wrist and in front and a jacket (called Chattai) open at the neck and the borders trimmed with lace. When they go about they throw over their head either a long piece of muslin (called Tuppatti) or a printed calico (called Malaya) which serves as a veil.

The dress of the poor sort generally consists among the men of only a short piece of cloth disposed of at the waist and among the women of a long one wrapped round the body and hanging down low enough to conceal the knees. In some parts of the country it is customary for the women of the lower orders, to have no covering over their girdles, so that their bosoms are entirely exposed. It would be too tedious to describe the various ornaments which are worn by the Tamils and I shall therefore notice only the principal kinds commencing with those of the men.

1. **Ottu.** An ear-ring worn by men by all ranks. It consists of a small ring of gold with a diamond or precious stone set in a case which is appended to it.

2. **Kadukkan.** A large kind of ear-ring. There are Kadukkans of different patterns, each having a distinct name, such as **Chetti-Kadukkan,**

CHARACTER CUSTOMS AND HABITS

Suttoo Kadukkan, Arippuchari Kadukkan, Urittiratcha Kadukkan and **Pulimuha Kadukkan.** The first is composed of a ring of about 10 or 11 inches in circumference with gold wire of great fineness chastely twisted over it, having either a pearl or precious stone fixed in the middle. Five or six of these rings are worn in each ear by the chetties of Colombo. The second is merely a ring of an oval shape. The third has little flower buds of gold threaded on gold wire. The fourth is set with the berries of the **Eleocarpus lancolotus.** The fifth has the figure of a tiger's face embossed in front.

3. **Murugu,** a little carving for the upper part of the ear having drops of pearls or emeralds suspended from it.

Men of quality wear in the gala days a variety of sarappali or gold chains and Padakkam or breast plates around their necks. They also usually have about their waist a string (called Areignan) made of twisted gold or silver wires and about their toe a plain silver ring (called **Minchi**). Boys wear collars (called **Karei**), either of gold or silver with a concave plate of the same metal resembling a moon hanging from the middle.

CHARACTER CUSTOMS AND HABITS

The ornaments of the females are as under specified.

1. **Kuppi.** An ornament of gold of the size of a walnut fastened to the tuft of hair in the head. It is beautifully engraved in circles and is often studded with precious stones.

2. **Sutti.** A gold strap, about four inches long, placed on the crown of the head hanging down the forehead in a line with the nose.

3. **Sinukki.** A flat piece of gold with a chain attached to it in each extremity and being hooked to one of the ear-rings is fixed in the knot of hair in a diagonal direction so as to compress the hair and keep it in front of the head.

4. Porei
5. Poludu } Two gold jewels in the form of the crescent moon and the sun also fixed to the hair fronting each other.

6. **Pattam.** A flat piece of gold tied at the forehead.

7. **Mookutti.** A gold knob which lies flat on the left side of the nose with a pearl or precious stone hanging from it.

8. **Nattu.** A gold pendant hanging from the Septum sometimes contains three rubies and one pearl and it nearly touches the upper lip.

9. **Todu.** A round ear-ring studded in front with precious stones and fastened into the lower aperture of the ear. It has sometimes drops of pearls hanging when it is called **Tulukkya.**

10. **Koppu.** A gold ear-ring worn in the upper part of the ear. It is of various shapes but, generally has a jointed head in the form of a cone, with a circular plate at the bottom, garnished with rubies or pearls.

11. **Nagapadam.** An ear-ring fixed below the **Koppu** with the device of a serpent's head.

12. **Mani** or beads. It is not possible to determine the number of the strings of gold beads worn by Tamil women. It depends entirely in the degree of affluence they possess. The beads are of different descriptions and distinguished after the names of the flowers or fruits to which they are made to resemble. Sometimes the beads are alternately strung with perforated corals or pearls.

13. **Chavadi.** A necklace resting on the shoulders.

14. **Attigei.** A necklace set with rubies, fastened tight to the neck.

15. **Ulkattu,** similar to the former but it is seldom bedecked with any precious stones.

16. **Tali.** An ornament which the bridegroom hangs on the neck of the bride on the day of marriage. It consists of a circular piece of gold, fastened either by a gold string or a string of cotton dyed yellow with turmeric. The Hindus engrave on it the probosis and pendant belly of Pulleiyar and the Christians the figure of a dove implying the descent of the deity in this form on the occasion of our Saviour's baptism in the Jordon.

17. **Nelie.** Two gold or silver wires twisted together somewhat like a puzzle ring and worn above the elbow.

18. Kappu, 19. Kankanam, 20. Valaiyel, 21. Sari, 22. Kadagam.	Different sorts of gold or silver rings and bracelets worn below the elbow. The rings are generally gold but the bracelets are formed globular and hollow and more than an inch in diameter,

23. **Ottiyanam.** A gold or silver girdle worn over the chela to keep it fast.

24. **Tandei.** Large convex hoops of silver within which are enclosed little pebbles which tinkle: and they are worn above the ankles.

25. **Sadangai** or Salangai. Large rings of silver with little balls of the same metal hung round them so as to make a tinkling noise. They are worn below the Tandei.

26. **Padagam.** Large silver chains like those which are fastened to the upper part of the branches of the bridle also worn at the ankles.

27. **Kolusu.** Similar to preceding

28. Nigamoodi
29. Peeli
30. Muntangi
31. Myladdi
32. Makarameen

} Different kinds of silver rings worn on the toes.

Both men and women wear on their fingers a great number of rings either of gold or silver and often garnished with gems or pearls.

As the ladies of the Chetties in Colombo differ from their sisters in the South of India in their costumes so they differ from them also in their decorations. On the head they have only a few gold bodkins (called **Penichi**) made in the form of arrows with which they fasten the braided hair behind; adding to them on some high occasion, a large bouquet of jewels like those described by Lady Worsley Montague to be in fashion with the Turkish women, and also a tortoise shell comb, the top of which is mounted with gold and bedecked with precious stones. On the upper part of the ear they have a **Kappu**, next to it a trinket (called **Krabu**), and five or six rings (called **Urukkumuni**) studded around with small globules of gold and below these three large solid pendants (called **Chavadi Kudukkan**) hanging as low as the shoulders. Neither on their foreheads nor on their nose have they any jewels but their neck, hands and feet are loaded with them.

With regard to the diet of the Tamils, it is admitted on all hands that they are in some degree abstemious. Among them the Brahmans and those of the superior classes who are punctilious in their adherence to the tenets of **Siva**, live entirely upon Vegetables and milk; their food consisting simply of boiled rice pulse, green gram, curries and pickles made of half ripe fruit curds, butter, and ghee. As to the other castes some confine themselves wholly to fish while others do not scruple to eat mutton, pork and goats flesh as well as every kind of bird that is not carniverous. The **Kuraver** and a few of the like wandering tribes include in the list of their diet armadillos, squirrels, cats, and land tortoises and the Parriahs feed even on the flesh of bullocks and buffaloes.

Though the use of intoxicating liquor is abhorred by the Brahmans and other superior classes yet it is a lamentable fact that almost the whole of the lower classes are addicted to it. The opinion that this vice was introduced by the Europeans is erroneous, for it was known among the Tamils long before their arrival and prevailed to a great extent chiefly among the men as well as women of the cultivating tribes, as will be seen by the following description of a festive scene translated from the **Nattu Padalam** a section of the Skanda Puranam.

"The plough women having filled the toddy in small cups looked at it as they were looking into a looking glass, and drunk greedily."

"Of those who drunk the toddy, some fainted, some were dejected, some groaned, some sang, some adored, and some danced."

"They become immodest, libidinous, groanful' and pensive and at last losing their senses they sank motionless. Is there anything more intoxicating than toddy ?"

"While they walked on the side of the transparent pools of water and the fields they reeled about and as there were none to lead them they did not proceed on. Have they any strength who are inebriated ?"

Both men and women chew betel and evince a particular liking for it. The use of tobacco has gained ground among them; though the Brahmans often inveigh against it, remarking that even the leaves of all the palmyrah trees in the world are not sufficient to write a book on its baneful effects.

Most of the cooking utensils of the Tamils are of earthenware. Among the Brahmans and Saivas, none of them are allowed to be seen by a person of low caste, and if a dog lick them they would be immediately broken. With some exceptions the Tamils do not use any plates, consequently their rice is served on a plantain leaf and the curries and pickles in leaves of the like kind but stitched to resemble cups. As they eat with their fingers they are like the Jews, very punctilious in washing their hands before as well as after and while at meal they sit down on the floor cross legged. In drinking water they pour it from a copper vessel (called Chembu) directly into the throat without letting it come in contact with their lips. The Brahmans and Saivas will never eat any thing which is cooked by a person of a different caste or religion or allow any but the members of their own family to go into their kitchen, and they leave off eating if the lamp before them is blown out by accident or anybody sneezes. An apparent change is however, perceptible in the habits of the Tamils in Ceylon especially of those residing in Colombo. They are, as we have already observed gradually approximating to the Europeans with whom they have intercourse. Instead of sitting cross legged on mats at meals as formerly, they now sit on chairs at tables. They no longer eat out of the same dish and their meals are served up with regularity and neatness. They have nevertheless not yet in general, adopted the use of spoons and forks or allowed the females to join in their parties.

CHAPTER X.

Of the mode of salutation and other usages of Society.

In common with other Hindu Nations the Tamils have many modes of salutation. When they meet a person of a superior rank they salute him by joining their hands and lifting them up to the forehead or breast or placing only the right hand upou the face in a longitudinal position saying, Tambiran Nanmei Taratum i. e. God confer on you good; when persons of equal rank meet, some simply bow to each other and some raise their joined hands to the breast.

The Brahmans are saluted by the other castes by elevating their joined hands over the head saying, Tendam Aiyah 'i.e. I worship you sir; The former reply, Aservadem i. e. Blessing be on you, extending their right hand towards the latter at the same time.

OF THE MODE OF SALUTATION ETC.

When the Tamils approach the person of a King or a pontiff, they prostrate themselves before him at full length, bringing the forehead, the chest, the two shoulders, the two hands and the two feet in contact with the ground.

A son salutes his father or mother by falling down and grasping the feet, but this mode of showing respect to parents is observed only on some particular occasion.

Kissing by way of salutation is not known among the Tamils. In some parts of Ceylon however, when relations meet together on the holy days or after a long separation they embrace each other and kiss on the cheek.

There are among the Tamils besides saluting sixteen different kinds of civility offered to superiors. Their enumeration is as follows:—

(1) Giving a seat, (2) giving water for the hands, (3) giving water for the feet, (4) giving water for bathing the body, (5) giving milk, the juice of sugar cane and the water of young cocoanuts, (6) assisting in putting on garments, (7) putting on the triple cord, (8) sprinkling perfumed water, (9) adorning with garlands, (10)

strewing rice coloured with turmeric, (11) offering incense, (12) getting up a lamp, (13) burning camphor, (14) furnishing food, (15) presenting betel, (16) worshipping and scattering flowers.

In the 39th chapter of the Casi Candam entitled **Illaram Kooriya Addhiyayam**, nine rules are required to be observed when one goes to visit another, namely (1) to pay him due respect, (2) to address him in courteous and pleasing language, (3) to receive him cheerfully, (4) to entreat him to advance, (5) to rise on his approach, (6) to entertain him with exhilarating discourse, (7) to attend assiduously by his side, (8) to accompany him for a space when he departs and (9) to treat him with the before mentioned sixteen kinds of civility during his stay.

When they walk with a person much superior to them in rank or caste they never go sidelong or before him and it will be considered extremely rude not to cast off their slippers, and lower down to the waist the shawl they have on their shoulders when they speak to him.

The Tamils have great reverence for their elders. They always rise from their seats when they see them and give them precedence in all their public as well as private assemblies.

It deserves notice that the Tamils in general address each other whether related or not, by the terms of relationship and Mr. Babington in a note to his translations of the Adventures of Guru Paramartham, P. 90 observes that in this respect they follow the rule of Erasmus "**Senes ignotos adolescentulos filiorum Cognomento Salutant adolescentes vicissum illos patres aut Dominos.**"

At public entertainments, such as are given on the occasions of a marriage or funeral the guests take their seats in several rows according to rank and seniority, and the host himself generally waits upon them and serves out the rice. None will rise and go aside before all have finished eating when they are presented with betel and dismissed.

Almost all the European writers on India speaking of the native females, describe their state as one of misery and imprisonment. I may however safely venture to contradict this statement as it regards the Tamils for they not only treat their women with respect but also allow them every liberty which is consistent with propriety. "In Southern India" says Mr. Ellis "the conduct of women is much less restrained than in the Northern provinces; their persons are not concealed, and they are allowed to partake of the business and amusements of their male relations. Those whose circumstances compel them to personal labor may be seen crowding the public wells and reservoirs and it is thought no disparagement even for those of higher station to bathe in the open tanks when they display admirable address in avoiding any indelicate exposure of their persons. At religious festivals, marriages, processions and other public shows and ceremonies the number of women of all ranks exceeds that of the men (*vide Commentary on the Cural p. 171*). Abbe Dubois, notwithstanding he has joined the writers who have charged the natives with using their females ill "That they (the females) receive the highest respect in public." "A woman," says he, "may go wheresoever she pleases, she may walk in the most public places and have nothing to fear from libertines numerous as they are in the country. A man who should stop to gaze on a woman in the street or elsewhere, would be universally hooted as an insolent and a most lowbred fellow."

“(vide Description of India, Ch: xviii, p. 220). It is true that among certain castes of the superior grade the females feel some delicacy to mingle in general society, and on that account keep themselves within doors, but they do not, however scruple to appear in public when occasion requires or to converse with their male friends and acquaintances. There are among the Tamils a great number of rules prescribed by their ancient writers for the conduct of women, the whole of which appear briefly summed up in the divine command given to our first mother "Thy desire shall be subject to thy husband and he shall rule over thee," Gen. Ch. III 16.

CHAPTER XI.

Of the Rites and Ceremonies of the Tamils.

The rites and ceremonies which the Tamils as professors of the Hindu religion have to observe at certain epochs of their life are very numerous, and in describing them I shall commence with those observed on account of the females before and after their parturition.

The Tamils generally evince much anxiety when a woman is pregnant especially for the first time and supposing that in that state she is subject to many accidents by the malignant influence of evil spirits, or the evil eye. They practise on her at different intervals the three following ceremonies in order to prevent them. (1) **Garba Dhanam,** is performed as soon as the signs of pregnancy have manifested themselves. In this as in other occasions the whole house is cleaned in their fashion by besmearing the floor with cowdung and an image of the god Pilleiyar (Ganesa) is set up on a little mound of earth raised in the middle of the verandah. The Brahman who conducts the ceremony first breaks a cocoanut before the above image and presents it as a propitiatory offering to the God. He, then, kindles the **Homam** or sacrificial fire, feeding it with the dry sprigs of different trees, five grain, clarified butter etc., and reciting certain mantras (orisons) at the same time and when it is over pronounces a blessing on the pregnant woman, who in return offers him a donation consisting of money, cloth or cattle according to her means.

2. **Pumsavanam** is performed in the third month. It is conducted in the same manner as that above described, except that at its close females present practise on the pregnant woman the rite called **Arati** or **Alati,** by taking in their hands a basin of water coloured red with turmeric and chunam, and one after the other whirling it round her head three times and the father presents her with a pair of bangles.

3. **Simantam** is performed in the seventh month. The relations and friends of the pregnant woman being assembled under a **Pandal,**

erected for this purpose in the courtyard of her house each of them boils rice in three pots and offers it to the household gods and the manes. After this the woman arrayed in her wedding garments stands in the middle of the **Pandal** bending forward her body and resting her hand on a wooden mortar which is placed before her and the females who are related to her on the husband's side, take some milk in a spoon and in turn drop it on her shoulders. In some parts of the country it is usual on this occasion, to make her sip some holy water which is sent for from the temple. The whole is concluded with a repast and the guests, before they separate, each present the husband and the wife with a handful of betel leaves and some pieces of money.

During the time a woman is pregnant her husband refrains himself from shaving his beard and often observes certain periodical fasts.

Two or three days previous to the expected time of delivery the pregnant woman is removed to a separate apartment in order to prevent the dwelling house from being defiled by her lying in it.

After child-birth the wife of a Brahman is unclean for eleven days, of a Kshatriya for 16, of a Vaisiya for 21; and of a Sudra for 31 days, and during this time she is neither allowed to mix with her family nor touch any cooking utensils in the house (Compare Lev. xii) when the term expires the ceremony of propitiation is perfomed in the following manner:— A mound of earth is raised in the middle of the verandah and being besmeared over with cow-dung is marked with stripes of white. Upon this mound are placed besides the image of Pilleiyar a plantain leaf with some raw rice on it, a dish containing a mixture of cow's urine and milk, and a jug of water wound with cotton thread, having on the top a cocoanut straked with turmeric and ornamented with chaplets of mango leaves. The mother places herself before the mound holding the child in her arms and the Brahman who is now called to celebrate the ceremony after making an offering to Pilleiyar, consecrates the water in the jug and besprinkles the whole house with it besides dropping a little on the heads of the mother and the child. After this an entertainment is given to all who attended the accouchment especially the midwife and the laundress who are also paid their fees on this occasion. Among some castes the ceremoney of purification consists merely in besmearing the floor of the house with cowdung and making a rice offering to the household gods.

The following ceremonies are observed with regard to infants and young persons.

(1) **Jata Karman.** The ceremony of birth, which the father is required to attend to as soon as that event takes place. The principal part of it consists in presenting gingelly seed, gold, kine etc., to the Brahmans and washing himself and offering prayers to the Gods before he sees the child. When the umbilical cord is cut often, but not always, the relations and friends present throw some money into the basin of water in which the child has been previously washed and this with the instrument used in the operation is appropriated by the midwife as her perquisite.

At the birth of a child it is usual to consult an astrologer and get the child's **Jatakam** or horoscope written, which contains besides the child's birth the name of the stellar mansion in which the moon was at the time; the relative positions of the planets to the sun and the good or evil which will happen to the child by their influence through life.

2. **Nama Karnam.** Giving a name to the child, which is done on the tenth or twelfth day after its birth. Few take their children to temple for the purpose unless they have made a vow to that effect. Among the Brahmans it is conducted with great show, and includes a burnt offering to the nine planets in order to propitiate them. The other castes however, content themselves with breaking a cocoanut in honour of Pilleiyar and burning incense before his image. The name is generally given by the father, and as a part of the rite some ashes are rubbed on the child's forehead and besides pouring into its mouth a few drops of holy water.

3. **Karnam Vedanam.** Boring the child's ear; this is performed on the twelfth or sixteenth day after birth but it is frequently delayed till the 6th or 8th month and sometimes longer. The parents set up a pandal as in other solemnities, and invite all their friends and relations to be present when the ears are bored as well as to partake of an entertainment which is given afterwards in honour of the event. In Southern India the operation is performed by a goldsmith

if a male child or by a man of the Kurave tribe if a female.

4. **Annappirasanam,** Giving solid food; this is done in the 6th or 8th month but often after the lapse of a year and it is accompanied with a feast (compare Genesis 21. 8.) The Brahmans have a burnt offering made on the occasion; and the brass vessel out of which the child is fed for the first time and which the maternal uncle provides, is solemnly consecrated by writing several **mantras** over it before it is used for the purpose. At the close of the ceremony the child is girdled with a **Sittadei,** a little cloth, and taken to the temple and presented to the God.

When the first teeth appear it is customary among some castes to distinguish the occasion by distributing cakes decorated with the Kernel of the cocoanut cut in the form of small teeth.

5. **Chanulam.** The shaving the head of the child in its first or third year, constitutes the object of this ceremony. After the usual offerings to Pilleiyar are made the barber shaves off the child's hair leaving only a small tuft on the crown of the head, or near the forehead according

to the custom of the caste to which the child belongs. When this operation is finished the Brahman offers a burnt sacrifice to invoke the blessing of the Gods upon the ceremony which closes with a repast to all who have honoured it with their presence.

I should not omit to mention here, that in some parts of the country the young men are not allowed to shave their heads for the first time till a feast is made and the ceremony called **Urumalkattu** or tying the head cloth round their heads is performed; and this custom appears to bear some analogy to the **Juvenalisludi** instituted by Nero the first time his beard was shaved, and also to the rites observed among the Romans when the **toga virilis** was assumed by their young men at the age of seventeen.

6. **Viddhyarambam,** or sending a boy to school. In the families of the rich this event is celebrated with some pompous display. The relations and friends being assembled the school master is called in who, often making the usual offering to Pilleiyar writes out the alphabet (called **Ari Vari**) in three separate **olahs** which are rubbed over with turmeric and fumigated with incense, and then teaches the boy to recite

it three times. After this both the school master and the boy are paraded in a palankeen or on horse-back, accompanied by music, and an entertainment is given to all the guests.

The usual time for sending a boy to school is when he has attained his fifth year, and with regard to the course of studies pursued by the Tamils generally I beg to refer the reader to Captain Harkness' able remarks on the school system of the Hindus published in the first volume of the Jl. of the R. A. S.

Upanayanam. This ceremony is peculiar to the Brahmans, who observe it with great solemnity when a youth of their tribe is initiated into the sacerdotal society by investing him with the Poonool or triple cord, and whispering in his years the **Gayetri** or most mysterious text of the **Veda.** The parents are obliged to offer numerous burnt offerings and libations, to the household gods and the **manes** for three successive days and entertain all the Brahmans in the place and present them with sundry gifts on the fourth day. In a certain stage the youth has his head anointed and his whole body immersed in water, and after he undergoes these rites, he is considered as being born again. Hence the

Brahmans call themselves **Iruprappaler** or the twice born.

When a girl attains the age of puberty the Tamils in general observe the ceremony called **Samarthya-Kaliyanam** and keep her secluded in a retired part of the house for seven or eleven days. She is then bathed, on which occasion all her female friends and relations are invited to partake of an entertainment consisting of rice puddings and cakes. While the girl is bathing the women in attendance sprinkle each other with turmeric water and they subsequently perform the rite of Arati to protect her from the influence of the evil eye. In some parts of the country the married women who are related to the girl assemble at her house on the third day, and after making her undergo certain whimsical ceremonies, sing as they dance round her, clapping their hands.

CHAPTER XII.

OF THE RITES AND CEREMONIES OF THE TAMILS (Contd.)

The celebrations of marriage (called Vivaham or Kaliyanam) being considered by the Tamils as a matter of primary importance, the present chapter will be exclusively devoted to a minute discription of the various rites and ceremonies practised on the occasion according to the Tamil authors who have written on the subject. There were formerly eight different modes of conducting the marriage ceremony viz :

1. Bramam
2. Prajappattiyam
3. Aridam
4. Deivam

In these four the bride was given to the bridegroom by the father or the relations.

5. **Gandarvam**

In this the parties of themselves formed the union without the knowledge or consent of their parents or relations.

6. Asuram

In this the bridegroom was obliged to perform an act of prowess. A marriage rite similar to the above seems to have been known to the Hebrews as is proved by the circumstance of David giving one hundred foreskins of the Philistines for the daughter of Saul.

7. Irakkadam

In this the bride was seized by violence against her consent and that of her parents and relations.

8. **Paisasham.**

In this the bride was either forcibly taken away from her parents or violated while in a state of idiotism, asleep or intoxicated. Of all these modes of marriage that which is at present in vogue is the **Asuram** with some variation. Instead of the act of prowess on the part of the bridegroom a consideration money (called Parisam) varying in proportion to the rank and condition of the parties, has been substituted and this though paid into the hands of the bride's father is appropriated to her own use.

The rules for selecting a wife are enumerated in the Karma Puranam and I shall here subjoin a metrical version of them as given by Mr. Ellis in the commentaries on the Kural, p. 195.

Equal in rank and of a kindred stem,
But sprung not from the blood that flows in thine
And in thy father's veins should be thy bride;
Sweet as the fragrant beverage of the Gods
The cany juice or the honey of the boughs
Should flow her mild and softly lisping speech
And hers the beauteous face the due beamed moon
Displays, when with full orb she gilds the night
Wise as a prince's counseller must she be
A slave in needful toil; in beauty bright
As from the wave borne flower the goddess rose
Whose charms subdue the world, humble as seems

The all enduring earth ; in love mature,
As is the mother's breast ; in nuptial bliss
Free as the forest of the joyous choir
Whose wanton wiles allure the melting heart,
Though chaste as **Arundati** ; in her soul
The strictest points should dwell, her mein
The graceful **Urvasi**, who captivates
In heaven all eyes all minds should emulate ;
And high should rise the round and swelling hills
Her bosom bears ; with ardour such an one
In wedlock seek and give her all thy love.

Though it sometimes happens that the youngest sons or daughters are married first, yet this practice is strictly prohibited in the Vedas as will be seen by the following extract from the Casie Candam.

"If the younger should marry before the elder he would enter the fiery hell unless the elder is either dumb or deaf or has renounced the world."

So said Laban when Jacob offered to marry his youngest daughter. "It must not be so done in our country to give the youngest before the first-born. (*Gen* xxix. 26.)

Daughters are disposed of in marriage often ong before they attain the age of puberty and among the Brahmans it is considered a very heinous sin to allow their daughters to remain in a state of celibacy after they have completed their 12th year. In every case where the girl married is under age, she lives with her parents and is given away to the husband when she becomes fit to fulfil the duties of conjugal life.

Proposals of marriage are always made by the young man's father and before they are assented to, the young woman's father has the horoscopes of the two parties examined with regard to their correspondence with each other in the ten different astrological points (called Dasapporuttam) which is considered essential for a fortunate union.

When the match is approved of, the young man's father proceeds to the dwelling of the young woman with tom tom sounding before him and attended by his son and a few friends. He takes with him seven or nine bunches of plantain and some cocoanuts streaked with turmeric and after he has offered them to the young woman's father proposes and settles the amount of **Parisam** or dowry, which it should be remembered varies with the caste and condition of the parties. They then draw up a contract (called Pattolei) and fix the day for the celebration of the marriage. A great number of ceremonies are observed on this occasion and before the young man takes his leave the young woman's father often makes him a present besides feasting him and his attendants.

As the day appointed for the marriage approaches the fathers on each side commence erecting a **Pandal**, or booth in the Court-yard of their respective dwellings. In raising these **Pandals** disputes frequently arise touching the number of **Kals** or poles, required to support the horizontal roof, as none but those of the right hand castes are entitled to twenty one. The erection of the first pole on the North East side is accompanied by many superstitious observances and they always select for it the tree called Odhi or Odina Pinnata. Before it is fixed in the ground it is besmeared with pulverized Sandal, turmeric and red ochre and wrapped over with a circle of mango leaves and **Kusa** grass and when about to be put into the hole destined to receive it, they pour over it some milk mixed with paddy and cotton seeds and split a cocoanut into two equal parts as a propitiatory offering to Pilleiyar. The Pandal is hung with white cloth both inside and out or inside only and tastefully decorated with bunches of ripe arecanuts, cocoanut blossoms, leaves, and lanterns and flowers made of coloured paper, tinsel etc. In front of their dwellings they set up triumphal arches, adorning them with the cocoanut leaves and fix two rows of the stems of plantain trees with lamps on their tops, forming a street from the door of their habitation to the **Pandal.** In the centre of the **Pandal** erected at the dwelling of the bride an extra pole is fixed called **Arasanikal,** or the lady pole and near it is raised a small mound of earth on which is deposited a ball of cowdung ornamented with a few blades of Kusa grass to represent **Pilleiyar.** Opposite to the **Arasanikal** a square pit is dug and the inside besmeared with cowdung for the purpose of kindling the **Homam** or sacrificial fire. On its edge are placed a lighted lamp, and the figure of an elephant formed of clay and bearing on its back three or seven painted pots piled one over another, the uppermost of which has a cocoanut streaked with turmeric on the top.

When every necessary preparation is completed an invitation is given to all their relations and friends by presenting them each with betel. On the day of marriage as the guests assemble the bridegroom proceeds to the bride's house carrying with him the necklace (called **Tali**) and the garment (called **Koorei**) which he has to present her with. In the marriage of the rich, the bridegroom sets out either in a palanquin or on horseback, the washerman spreads white cloth along the road, two others fan him with **Chamarams** or whisks, while four persons hold a canopy over his head or palanquin; the musicians follow with their music; two barbers blow chanks, dancing girls move in measure; and a number of boys carry lighted torches, white umbrellas, flags and other insignia of his caste.

As soon as the bridegroom is seen approaching, a party of the married women present go out to hail him with the ceremony of **Arati**, as it has been described elsewhere, and when he enters the pandal, he is presented by the bride's mother or sister with a cup of bruised plantains and milk and placed on a raised seat in the middle of the Pandal. The bride who all the while has remained in the inner apartment, being now arrayed in her splendid apparel, is carried to the temple in a palanquin with the sound of tom tom and other marks of respect and made to undergo some superstitious rites, after which she is ushered into the Pandal and seated by the side of the bridegroom upon the mound of earth, both keeping their faces directed towards the East. The guests then take their respective places and the Brahman after tying a yellow thread (called **Kankanam**) round the right arm of the bridegroom and another round the left arm of the bride proceeds to perform the rites by which they are to be constituted husband and wife. He commences with an offering to Pilleiyar and ignites the sacrificial fire in the square pit near the mound occasionally throwing into it handfuls of each sort of fine grain and a number of dried sprigs of the trees* Al (1) Arasu (2) Itti (3) Atti (4) Ma (5) and Karunkali (6) together with the kusa grass and (7) Naeyurivi plant, also pouring into it drops of clarified butter 108 times at different

(1) Ticus benghalensis (2) Ticus religiosa
(3) „ vireaus (4) „ racemosa
(5) Mangifora indica (6) Diospyros ebenum
(7) Achyranthus asfora

intervals ; reciting each time a formula from the **Veda**, and a series of short prayers, the intention of which is to invoke the deities to accept the sacrifice thus offered and to endow the couple about to be married with happiness and prosperity. At this stage of the proceedings the Tali is produced by the bridegroom's sister and the Brahman receiving it from her offers incense to it and hands it round to the guests each of whom touches it successively. The Bridegroom then taking the necklace places it round the bride's neck and his sister who waits behind him fastens it properly. While this is being done, the married women present put some paddy and betel into a seer, measure, which they whirl round the heads of the happy pair thrice, and the Brahman divides the cocoanut which lay on the painted pot into two equal parts.

When the above ceremony is ended, the rite called **Panikraham** is performed by the Brahman which is that of putting the little finger of the bridegroom's left hand round the little finger of the bride's right hand describing a pottu or circle on their foreheads with pulverized sandal and the sacrificial ashes, and making them afterwards circumambulate the fire pit three times from left to right throwing into it handfuls of paddy mixed with flowers etc., as they pass. These circumvolutions having been performed the Brahman pronounces the following sentences "The sun and moon, the fire and the three hundred and thirty three millions of gods are witnesses, that——the son of—— now gives his daughter——as wife to—— who is the son of——," upon which the father ——takes the hand of his daughter and puts it into that of his son-in-law, and pours water over them repeating at the same time the above declaration.

After this the married couple resume their seats on the mound of earth and their relations and friends chant a blessing on them, wishing them numerous progeny and long life in the following words: "You shall flourish like the Banian tree, and take root like the kusa grass, you shall shoot up like bamboo and live without end." (compare Psalm CXXVII).

The people then withdraw for the day not however partaking of an entertainment.

Next day early in the morning the bridegroom goes in procession to the temple and presents an offering to the God. In the evening the bridegroom and the bride are seated in a

Palanquin with their faces towards each other and paraded through all the principal streets of the town, when the relations hail them with the ceremony of **Arati** and present them with a cup of bruised plantains and milk as they pass their houses.

Upon returning home the bride's brother washes the feet of the bridegroom who in return puts a ring on his finger. The Brahman then consecrates some **Gingelly** oil, of which a part is given to the barber and the washerman in waiting, and with the other part the bride's brother anoints the head of the bridegroom, and the bridegroom's sister that of the bride ; and therefrom they are conducted to a well and bathed, the bridegroom standing with one end of the bride's cloth about his loins and she with the other. After the ceremony of bathing is thus concluded the bride retires to her closet, but the bridegroom remains in the Pandal where his father-in-law and every one of the guests present him with three handfuls of betel and a sum of money according to their means. On the third day the Brahman is again called in and an oblation of rice boiled with milk is offered to the sun. The bride then treads on a grinding stone with the tip of her right foot, while the bridegroom points out to her through an aperture made in the roof of the Pandal the star **Beta** in the tail of **Ursa Major** saying "Lo! there is Aruntudi the consort of **Vashista** a pattern of matrimonial chastity." This being done the Brahman taking a muller, besmeared with turmeric and wrapped in a silk cloth, and waving it over the sacrificial fire presents it to the bridegroom who hands it over to the bride saying "Here is thy child." The muller is called in Tamil **Kulavi** which also signifies a child. The assembled guests then severally offer her a piece of money and sprinkle both her and the bridegroom as well as themselves with turmeric water, and afterwards sit down to a dinner of which the bride and the bridegroom also partake, eating together from the same plate as a token of their close union.

The bride is conducted to the husband's house on the fourth day; but in case she is under the age of puberty, she remains with her parents until she has attained that age.

On the seventh day, the bridegroom pays a formal visit to his mother-in-law, accompanied by the bride as well as all his friends and relations, carrying with him a present consisting of seven or nine pots of cakes, and an equal number of cocoanuts streaked with turmeric. As he approaches the house of the mother-in-law she advances to meet him, and, having performed the rite of Arati on him, conducts him and his party into the house where an entertainment awaits them. He remains there the whole day, and takes his leave in the evening.

It must be observed here that among the Brahmans the marriage rites are observed for a second time when the husband shall have attained the age of sixty years; these sexagesimal weddings, however, have seldom taken place in Ceylon as far as I could ascertain.

Among **Karreyar** or fishing tribes, especially in the district of Puttalam, three different forms of marriage prevail, which appear to vary much from those already described.

The first, called **Maleimanam** is performed by the bridegroom's sister simply hanging the **tali** round the neck of the intended bride after decking her person with wreaths of certain flowers and anointing her with certain odours.

When thus married, if either party disagree or do not wish to live together they may part after the payment of a fine of twenty five Rix dollars to the temple by the party who desires a separation.

The second is called **Sirutali** which is nothing more than hanging the tali as aforesaid without any ceremonies whatever; and in this case the party desiring to be divorced is obliged to pay a fine of twelve Rix dollars and six fanams to the temple.

The third is called **Manjel Poosal**, viz, contracting the marriage without even hanging the **Tali**: the bridegroom's sister merely besmears the bride's garment with pulverized turmeric, and in this case the party who wishes to be divorced is only obliged to pay a fine of six Rix dollars and three fanams to the temple. Though the Tamil Christians in their marriage do not observe any one of the ceremonies which relate to the worship of the Gods, they retain yet the processions, and custom of hanging of the **Tali** round the neck of the bride, considering the latter in the same light as the Europeans do the presenting of a ring to the bride in the solemnisation of matrimony.

CHAPTER XIII.

OF THE RITES AND CEREMONIES OF THE TAMILS (Contd.)

Having endeavoured in the previous chapter to describe the ceremonies attendant on the marriages of the Tamils I shall now attempt to represent those observed in their funeral.

When a man is in the last extremity, the relations send for a Brahman, who after reciting some mantras or orisons, pour into his mouth a little of the Panchakariyum or mixture of cow's urine and milk etc., which is consecrated for the occasion with much solemnity. The sick man is then made to grasp a cow by the tail and afterwards present her to the Brahman as a sin offering. As death approaches his head is placed towards the North and one of the bystanders repeats aloud in his ear the name of Siva three times marking his forehead and breast with holy ashes at the same time.

When life is extinct the event is made known to the community by blowing a chank, and the females collected together squatting around the corpse put their arms on each other's shoulders and in a kind of recitative (called Oppari) bewail the loss of their friend. A Pandal is then erected in the courtyard of the house upon four poles and the corpse being washed after rubbing on the head some gengelly oil and expressed Illippe seeds is habited in a new garment and allowed to lie in state on a bed in the middle of the Pandal. When the people are assembled the corpse is placed either on a **Padei** (a sort of litter made of the branches of the cocoanut tree) or **Tandigei** (a splendid description of palanquin about six feet long, three broad and in the centre about four feet in height and ornamented with silken tassels) and carried to the place of burning, head foremost, upon men's shoulders, preceded by a person bearing fire in a vessel. All the male relatives and friends follow the bier with their heads uncovered and as they advance it is customary to halt in the way at different intervals and scatter parched rice mixed with cotton seeds and **Atti** leaves, as well as pieces of money. The funeral pile of the rich is composed of sandal wood but the poor have theirs commonly of firewood or dried cowdung and it is about four or five feet in height. When the body is laid on the pile it is covered over with a cloth and each of the nearest relatives present drops on the mouth a few grains of rice and a piece of money. The son or heir-at-law of the deceased then has his head shaved and performs the last peculiar rite of breaking the pitcher, which is this: he marches thrice round the pile with a pitcher of water on his shoulders and breaks it at the head of the corpse by gently suffering it to fall down. After this he takes a torch and applies the fire to the pile with his face turned in another direction and returns to his house; and those who remain to see the corpse burnt throw clarified butter and oil on the fire to hasten its consumption.

All who attended the funeral are considered unclean, and before returning to their houses or partaking of any food must wash their persons and clothes.

The female relatives and friends of the deceased meet together by his late residence, every morning and evening for the first eight days and there make a wailing. The son or heir-at-law who lighted the pile is obliged to fast for three days and nights, if he can, or otherwise eat a single meal at night, abstaining from salt and butter and, though not enjoined in the Vedas, yet it is customary for him not to pay visits, or attend to any business for sixteen days. He however makes no alteration in his dress, except on the day of funeral, when he, as well as the other relations, put on a piece of unbleached cloth as a token of their mourning.

Females who die in childhood and children under the age of seven years are not allowed to be burnt ; consequently their corpses are consigned to the earth after the foregoing ceremonies have been observed on them.

It should be here remarked that the corpses of the Sanniyasis or devotees are disposed of in the following manner. When a Sanniyasi dies his disciples dig a grave in the form of a well about six feet deep, and having lowered the corpse into it in a sitting position, fill it up with salt and raise a mound over it (called Samadi) and set up a **Lingam** over it which being consecrated by a Brahman becomes an object of worship, and offerings are made to it at stated periods. Before filling up the grave, however, a number of cocoanuts are broken on the head of the deceased and continued till the cerebrum comes out, the people who are collected together to witness it picking up every bit of the cocoanuts which they consider as an important relic. Subsequent to the obsequies, a great number of ceremonies are observed at different intervals for the repose of the soul of the deceased and I shall notice them here in the order they occur.

On the third day after the burning the relations and friends of the deceased proceed to the place where the body was burnt and offer a libation of water and gengelly seed accompanied with several oblations to fire of different kinds of parched grain, dressed on the spot for him. This being concluded the son or heir-at-law gathers the half calcined bones which remain and puts them into a copper vessel, and the Brahman who is in attendance, takes a branch of the **mango** tree and dips it in milk and sprinkles the whole three times. The bones are then carried and thrown into a river, or at other times kept in some safe place till an opportunity shall occur for sending them to the Ganges.

On the sixteenth day after the burning or burial, the house in which the deceased drew his last breath is purified by the observance of certain ceremonies called **Andiyetti**, and the relations meet to eat together.

At the expiration of forty days, or sometimes before or later as it suits the convenience of the parties, it is incumbent on the sons or heirs-at-law of the deceased to apply to the Brahman and have the ceremonies called **Karmandiram** performed for the repose of his soul. They are as follows:—a **Pandal** is erected in a solitary garden upon four poles, decorated with white cloths, green boughs and flowers. Under this **Pandal** the Brahman selects a level space, besmearing it with cowdung and forming squares on it similar to a chess table with various coloured powders. Nine copper vessels called chemboo piled one over the other and wound round with silk are placed near these squares and a cocoanut streaked with turmeric is laid on the top of the upper vessel. After the vessels are thus arranged the Brahman makes an effigy of **Kusa grass** and places it on a bier of the same material; all of which being concluded the relations bring out from the house of the deceased a triangular piece of brick, which was consecrated to the deceased on the night preceding, under a canopy of white cloth, accompanied by music of all sorts, chanks, tom-toms etc., and place that also near the squares. A wooden mortar and pestle are put at the entrance of the Pandal, which some one of the relations beats at intervals during the whole period of this external form of their religion. The son or heir-at-law has a string put across his shoulder, and wears a ring of **Kusa grass** on the little finger of his right hand; neither of which he can remove until everything is concluded, as they are considered symbols of his having bound himself by oath to conduct them. When all these preliminaries are adjusted, the Brahman kindles the sacrificial fire in a manner similar to that which is practised on occasions of marriage and after making oblations of rice mixed with milk curds and butter, the effigy is burnt and the ashes carefully gathered up and thrown into a tank. They then return to the **Pandal**, and forming a procession convey the piece of brick already mentioned to a river or any running water and there throw it in after which they immerse themselves in the same water once or twice, and return to their respective dwellings in their wet clothes.

The ceremonies for the dead do not end there. The surviving relatives continue to offer certain oblations in memory of the deceased on the anniversary of his death and those that have lost their fathers fast on every new moon, and those that have lost their mothers on every full moon.

The Tamil Christians still retain in some degree their funeral **Pandals** and processions and likewise abstain from eating as long as the corpse remains in the house, keep awake, make wailings and feed the poor at stated periods.

A woman is constituted a widow on the third day after the death of her husband, when the **Tali** is taken off from her neck by the near female connections. Among the Brahmans and a few other high castes, it is customary for widows to shave their heads and not to marry a second time. In the **Casi Candam**, the widows in general are allowed neither to braid up their hair nor stain their faces with the yellow dye of the turmeric nor to chew betel; but very few however now observe these rules, though they lay aside some of their ornaments. Both the Hindus and Christians regard the presence of widows at a marriage solemnity as an evil omen and consequently do not invite them on such occasions.

CHAPTER XIV.

OF THE RELIGION & SUPERSTITIONS OF THE TAMILS.

If we except a few thousands who have been converted to Christianity since the days of Xavier and Ziegenbalg, the bulk of the Tamils profess the Hindu religion and belong to either of the two grand sects into which it is divivded. It is said that they had once embraced **Buddhism** when that creed was predominant in the south of India; but none are to be found belonging to it at the present time, and the nation at large seems to have a very strong prejudice against it, not only on account of its atheistical principles but also as a cunning device of Vishnu to seduce the ancient inhabitants of Benares from their attachment to Siva.

The Hindu religion has been so ably illustrated by European writers that I consider it unnecessary to touch upon it here, and will therefore proceed to notice their superstitions.

Like every native living beyond the pale of Christianity the Tamils are in general extremely superstitious. They observe not only omens and lucky and unlucky days but also believe in ghosts and evil spirits and practise a number of whimsical ceremonies to keep them off.

Of all the birds of omen none strikes so much consternation in them as the owl. When he happens to alight on the roof of a house and begins to screech it is said to portend approaching death of one of the inmates. The kingfisher by the harsh noise he makes gives warning of some quarrel between friends and when one hears it he spits three times on the ground. The sight of a hawk or kite flying from left to right towards the South, or of the long tailed blackbird, from right to left towards the North, indicates good fortune; but the latter they say very seldom occurs. The croaking of the crow depends on the time to prove either good or bad, as the chirping of the lizard is on the diretion from which it proceeds. It is usual to snap one's finger on hearing a lizard chirp.

The following is a list of the good and bad omens to be met on the road as a person goes out of his house on a journey.

The good omens are:—a virgin, a prostitute, ripe fruits, ascetics, an elephant, a bull, a lion, a married woman, a washerman, ghee, milk, a full pot, boiled rice, meat and toddy.

The bad omens are :—a person with dishevelled hair, a person with a bald or shaved head, a mendicant, a sanniyasi, a solitary Brahman, a woman without breast, a person without a nose, a bundle of firewood, a hermophrodite, a valetudinarian, a barber and an one eyed person. If a dog happen to mount the top of a house or a cobra capella to enter one's bedroom on the fifth day of the moon's age it is considered as an evil presage, and the inmates forthwith quit the house and do not reoccupy it till certain propitiatory ceremonies shall have been performed and donations made to the Brahmans.

With regard to lucky and unlucky days the Tamils consult a work called **Ullamudei Chintamani** and punctiliously adhere to the rules it lays down in solemnising marriage, weaning a child, shaving the head, physicking the sick, building a house, changing residence, setting out on a journey and reaping corn etc.

In building a house, besides consulting the lucky time to lay the foundation, they also observe some rules as to its lucky or unlucky position, and those form the subject of a science—**Maneiade Satram.** Before they occupy a house they make offerings to Pilleiyar, and invoke his blessings upon it. The building of boats and vessels is also under certain superstitious rules (called **Navan Satram**) in reference to their size and shape, and as the boat wrights must conform to them without deviation, they scarcely aim at any improvement.

Connected with the foregoing superstitions is their observance of the **Rahu Kalam,** or certain parts of the day under the influence of the moon's nodes, and which is considered the most inauspicious period to undertake any important business or wait on a superior. This influence of the Rahu is supposed to continue only 3¾ **Naligei** or Tamil hours every day and to commence on

Sunday at	26¼	Naligei	after	sun	rise
Monday	3¾	,,	,,	,,	,,
Tuesday	22½	,,	,,	,,	,,
Wednesday	15	,,	,,	,,	,,
Thursday	18¾	,,	,,	,,	,,

Friday	11¼	Naligei after sun rise
Saturday	7½	" " " "

Travellers observe another superstition called **Soolam** or the indications of the trident in the hand of Siva and which he continually revolves through the different points of the compass, once every week, viz. on Monday and Saturday, towards the East for eight naligeis from sun rising; on Thursday towards the South for twenty naligeis from sun rising; on Friday and Sunday towards the West for twelve naligeis from sun rising; and it is ominous to travel in the direction it points.

The strange coincidences in dreams that frequently occur have so far confirmed the Tamils in their belief of them, that it is impossible to undeceive them of their delusion. They have like the "truth telling" gypsy of North Briton, a sort of key to the dreams (called **Kanavu Nool**) and to this they refer for an explanation of the scenes of their sleeping hours. Should the dream portend evil the dreamer makes offerings to the Brahman besides bestowing alms or the **Pandarams** and other religious mendicants and bathes himself in holy water.

The following is an extract from the **Kanavu Nool** or key to the dreams alluded to—

"To dream about the sun, moon, the gods, a mountain, sea, river, well, money, gold, precious stones, father and mother, child, grey headed matrons, elephant, horse, (car) bull, temple, Brahman, lotus, meat, ripe fruits, flower tree, swan, deer, clouds, fowl, honey, toddy, spirits, flowers, ashes, buttermilk, cotton, cobra capella, white colour and dead body or a lamp prognosticate good."

"To dream that he grasped with his hands either the sun or moon; or that a white cobra capella bit him on his right shoulder; or that he cut off its head and threw it on the ground, he will become a king."

"To dream that he sees a beautiful woman clad in white garments, enter his house, or that his house is on fire, he will become rich, and that he sees a chank, a full pot, a white umbrella or the deep river, or that he is offering to Pilleiyar, he will have great felicity."

"To dream that a virgin, holding a vessel in her hand falls from the heaven; or that the sun or moon is grasped by the serpent (i.e. eclipsed) he will have good grace with the king."

" To dream that the gods sing, laugh, dance, weep or clap their hands, or that he sees a sow, eagle, hawk, black cobra capella, ass, jackal, hog or monkey, he will meet with great evil."

"To dream about butter, milk, cotton, lions, firewood or red flowers portends adversity."

" To dream that either the sun or moon, stars, the flagstaff of steeple of a temple, or his own teeth fall, or that he loses his sight or hair, he will meet with great loss."

Next to dreams comes their belief in the **Kanoor** or baneful effects of the evil eye. This is a source of disquietude to a Tamil mother, who considers that every ailment of her child arises from it and will therefore never allow any individual, who is reputed to have evil eyes to visit her nursery. The ceremony of **Arati** which I have described in a former chapter has been instituted to soothe the qualms of mothers on this score from its supposed virtue to obviate the effects of the evil eye. It is also usual for gardeners to place on the trees or over the gate a white spotted pot, or the scull of a dead buffalo to attract the attention of the passengers from the trees to those objects that the trees may not suffer from evil glances.

Magic is not unknown to the Tamils. A great number of them profess to be adepts in this far famed art and exercise considerable influence over the ignorant masses of the people, who dread them more than they would the invisible spirits, with whom they are said to be familiar. The means which those magicians employ to cure dreams, or bring them on to infuse a devil into the body of any one or expel him and discover thieves, stolen property, or hidden treasure are various; but the limits of this work are too circumscribed to admit even a brief description of them. I shall, however, subjoin here an extract from Mr. Robert's oriental illustrations of the scriptures, containing an account of the mode of consulting familiar spirits as practised by the Tamil magicians, and which the reader will find bears a very striking resemblance to a similar practice noticed by Mr. Lane, in his account of the modern Egyptians, Vol I. p. 341, 357.

"A man who is in distress and who has resolved to consult a familiar spirit sends for two magicians; the one, is called the **Mantheravathe** i. e. he who repeats the incantations; the other the **Anjanam Parkeravan** i. e. he who looks and who answers to the questions of the former. His hand is rubbed with the **Anjanam** which is made of the burnt bones of the sloth, and the skull of a virgin; and when the ceremonies have commenced he looks steadily into his hand and can never wink or take off his eyes till all shall be finished.

"On the ground are placed rice, cocoanuts, plantains arecanuts, betel leaves, milk, camphor, and frankincense. The chief magician then with a loud voice begins to invoke the nine gods—Amman, Pulliar, Scandan, Aiyenar, Veerapatteran, Anjana, Anuman, Viraver. He then falls to the earth (as do all present) nine times and begins to whisper and "mutter" whilst his face is in the "dust", and he who looks in the hand "peeps" and stares for the beings who have to appear. All then stand up and the first wizard asks the second "what do you see"? He replies "my hand is cracked, has opened and I see in the ground." "What else do you see"?—"All around me is light. Come, Pulliar, come." He comes! He comes! His person, shape and dress are then described. The other eight gods are now entreated to appear, and as they approach the second person says 'They come' and they are invited to be seated in the places prepared for them."

"The first magician then enquires of the assembled gods what is the cause of the affliction, adversity or danger, of the person for whom the ceremony has been instituted. He who "peeps" in the hand then replies, and mentions the name of the evil spirit who has produced all the mischief. The malignant troubler is summoned to appear and to depart, but should he refuse, he is bound and carried off by the gods."

The maigcians are said to bring in diseases in a person by procuring his hair or nails and burying them with his effigy, after repeating some incantations over them both. Under the Tamil Kings those who practised this kind of magic were punished when detected, by having the two front teeth of their upper jaw drawn out, which prevented them from exercising their infernal art for the future.

The Tamils ascribe nearly all their misadventures and affections to the agency of evil spirits, who they say, have, however, more power in the night than in the day. There are evil spirits for every age and condition and those that plague the youth of both sexes are called **Mohini** which in some respect resemble the elms of ancient Briton. It is not uncommon to see men as well as women and children wearing about their waists or arms certain written spells (called **Atcharam**) enclosed in cylindrical cases of gold, silver or copper as preservatives against the evil spirits; and when these expedients fail they have recourse to sacrifices which are made to the evil spirits themselves in order to propitiate them. The evil spirits are supposed to reside chiefly in the margosa or banyan trees as well as in desolate houses and temples.

While I am on this subject, I must not omit to mention, that the propagation of small pox is attributed to **Mari Amman**, who though reckoned among the evil spirits yet is generally ranked with the principal divinities, she being an incarnation of Parvati, the consort of **Siva**. When the disease breaks out in a village and continues to rage for some time, the inhabitants seek to propitiate this goddess by means of bloody sacrifices and other offerings, and also place her image on a car and carry it about with great solemnity through the streets for three successive nights. Her priests (called Poosaris) likewise perambulate the village every day bearing a pot on their heads decked with margosa leaves and when they happen to pass by a house the inmates run out to meet them and pour water on their feet. The Tamils also are afraid of ghosts. As I have stated before they believe that the spirits of those who come to an untimely end wander on earth and frequently haunt their former dwellings.

Charms and spells for elephants, bears, tigers, and snakes are numerous and they constitute another inexhaustible source of the superstitions of the Tamils

REMARKS ON THE LANGUAGE AND LITERATURE OF THE TAMILS.

The Tamil language has been justly considered one of the most copious and elegant in the Eastern hemisphere, and is classified in the **Nigandu** under the head of "eighteen original tongues" of the **terra cognita** of the Hindus.

Some writers, amongst them Fra Bartolommeo, suppose it to be a dialect of the Sanskrit, but this is obviously an error; for "its peculiar structure, wholly dissimilar from Sanskrit, its deficiency in aspirated consonants, its possession of letters and sounds not found in Sanskrit, its division into dialects, one of which contains but few words of Sanskrit derivations and lastly, its locality at the Southern extremity of India would seem to indicate an independent origin, and one of at least equal antiquity with the Sanskrit itself."—*Transactions of the Royal Asiatic Society, vol II. p. 264.*

THE LANGUAGE AND LITERATURE

The Tamil language is divided into two dialects, viz. **Shen Tamil**, or high dialect and **Kodun Tamil**, or low dialect. The former comprises three further divisions, of which the first is termed **Eyet Tamil**, prose Tamil; the second **Issei Tamil**, poetical Tamil; and the third **Nadaga Tamil**, dramatic Tamil.

The Alphabet consists of twelve vowels and eighteen consonants, and, like the Greeks, the Tamils ascribe the invention of the whole of them to the gods.

No language in India, if we except the Sanskrit, can rival the Tamil in grammatical accuracy. To **Agastya** it is chiefly indebted for its high state of refinement, and as that philosopher happened to dwell on the mountain called **Podiyamalei**, in the south of the Peninsula, and was on that account addressed by the title of **Dekshana Moorti**, or the sage of the south, it has hence obtained the name of **Then Mohlie**, or the southern dialect. **Agastya** was the first who framed rules concerning the Tamil grammar, but in the lapse of time they have been lost; after his time several persons wrote on the subject, but their works have likewise perished, excepting the one by **Tolkappiyen**, who was one of the disciples of **Agastiya.** This, however, from its studied brevity, has been rendered scarcely intelligible, which led **Pavanandi Vidwan,** at the request and during the reign of the king **Siyagangen** of Madura to write a commentary upon it under the title of **Nunnool,** i.e. *Literae humaniores.* Beschi, speaking of this production observes that "although every one is familiar with the title, few have trod even on the threshold of the treatise itself." Though **Pavanandi Vidwan** had in his introduction to the Nunnool proposed to treat of all the five parts of the grammar, namely, Letters, Words, Matter, Versification, and Embellishment, he wrote only on the two first, and the defect was supplied by **Narkaviraja Nambi, Amirdasagaren** and **Tandi,** who each composed a treatise on a part. Different commentaries have been written on the Nunnool in modern times; but that which emanated from Beschi and called **Tonnool Vilakkam,** has thrown them all into the shade.

With regard to dictionaries, the Tamil language boasts of many, among which the one entitled **Nigandu,** the production of a Jaina king **Mandala Purusha,** is the best and most esteemed; like the **Amera Cosha,** it is composed in verse to be committed to memory, and is divided into twelve chapters, the contents of which are: 1st the titles of Deities, 2nd the names of Men, 3rd the names of Beasts, Fowls and Fishes, 4th the names of Plants, 5th the names of Places, 6th the names of Metals and Minerals, 7th the names of different objects, 8th and 9th names of Physical objects and actions, 10th the Verbs, 11th the synonymous words, 12th homonymous words.

The **Sadur Agaradi** by Beschi was chiefly compiled from this work and as he has arranged the words in Alphabetical order on the principle of European dictionaries, it has proved very useful to Tamil students.

It is a fact, attested by the numerous works, still in existence, on the liberal and mechanical arts, that the Tamils had made considerable progress in literature in the earliest period of their history. From the fourth century before, to the eleventh century after Christ, establishments for learning were in high repute amongst them, and there was a college at Madura, in which every literary production was received and approved. The kings of the **Chola** and **Pandiya** dynasties who then reigned over the Peninsula were themselves men of great learning, and made it a point to cherish and distinguish every genius by particular acts of munificence. The present generation, however, scarcely feel any desire to add to the stock, or improve it; and I doubt whether the Hindoo Literary Society of Madras by the mere printing and publishing of some MSS especially on Mythology, will ever be able to revive the national literature.